BENCHMARKING
Computer Evaluation
and Measurement

Edited by NICHOLAS BENWELL
School of Production Studies
Cranfield Institute of Technology
Bedford, England

HEMISPHERE
PUBLISHING CORPORATION
Washington, D.C.   London

A HALSTED PRESS BOOK

JOHN WILEY & SONS
New York   London   Sydney   Toronto

Hemisphere Publishing Corporation
1025 Vermont Avenue, N.W., Washington, D.C. 20005

Distributed solely by Halsted Press, a Division of John Wiley & Sons, Inc., New York.

Library of Congress Cataloging in Publication Data

Main entry under title:

Benchmarking: computer evaluation and measurement.

    Proceedings of a conference held at Churchill College, Cambridge, Eng., Oct. 1974.
    Bibliography: p.
    Includes indexes.
    1. Electronic digital computers—Evaluation—Congresses. I. Benwell, Nicholas.
QA76.5.B394   001.6′4′044028   75-14363
ISBN 0-470-06595-8

Printed in the United States of America

CONTENTS

PREFACE

Benchmarking '74 was a conference at which manufacturers, consultants, researchers, and others presented papers giving details of recent work in their individual fields. As a result, they viewed the subject from different perspectives, and this is apparent in the discussion sessions that have been included in this book.

I am grateful to the authors for their papers and also for vetting the transcripts. I have included all the amendments to accuracy that they picked up. Some of the tape recordings of what was said were difficult to follow, especially those recordings that included questions from the audience.

I have tried, as far as possible, to reproduce what was said in an almost Hansard form. I have removed what might well be necessary to somebody's lecturing style, like repetition and long-winded sentences, which certainly appeared superfluous to a written style. On the other hand, I have added the odd word or two that helped to make a passage clearer. Above all, I resisted the temptation to polish the prose too much; it would have been easy to make the style more formal, more elegant, always in the third person, and without the occasional colloquialism. If I had revamped the papers, the book would not contain a series of transcripts, and it might have been less readable, but, most important, I would not have told it like it was at Churchill College, Cambridge, in October '74.

NJB

An Introduction to
Benchmarking

Interest in the subject of benchmarking has been around for some years now. Wickens published a paper called, "A brief review of computer assessment methods," in 1968. Emery (1970, p. 140), in his well known textbook, refers to the subject as an established technique. So does Kilgannon in his book in 1972. It was a topic that seemed mainly to exercise the minds of researchers and organizers in such places as government departments, research centers, and universities. Generally, efforts in those days were confined to mathematical techniques to ensure that a computer installation was run as efficiently as possible (more details of these techniques follow). Attempts to investigate commercial installations, with such problems as variable workloads and intense data-base activity, seem almost unknown until the 1970s. Time-shared systems were becoming available during the 1960s, especially in the U.S.A., and in 1965 at The Massachusetts Institute of Technology Scherr published a Ph.D. thesis on the analysis of time-shared computer systems, but there is not much evidence of widespread interest until later.

As with many technical subjects, then, expertise and research papers were building up, more complex designs of computer were being sold, and the spread of computers into more and more commercial areas was being established. But benchmarking was still having little or no effect on the world of industry and commerce.

AMERICAN INTEREST

In the United States on June 6th, 1972, however, Temporary Federal Property Regulation Number E-23 was issued by the General

Services Administration of the Federal Government. This regulation includes the following clauses:

1. "A simulation input definition shall not be used as the only means of describing data processing requirements in solicitation documents. Such format shall be accompanied by a narrative description of the ADP objectives and the general logic diagrams when available."
2. "Solicitation documents shall not be construed in such a way as to require offerors/bidders to use a specific computer system simulator in order to offer/bid."
3. "Generally, offers/bids shall not be construed to be non-responsive or not acceptable solely on the basis of simulation results."

In the U.S.A., Federal Government automatic data processing (ADP) procurements must be carried out so that anybody who has a computer to sell or to lease can make a competitive bid. This is achieved by listing new system requirements in a Request for Proposals (RFP), which is the official advertising medium and is issued by the procuring agency. In order to obtain firm proposals for computer configurations, the functional and performance requirements must be specified by the RFP in detail. In addition, as computer requirements change rapidly, augmentations that would fit neatly into existing and future product ranges need to be specified so that vendors can respond to those changing requirements.

When the submissions are received they are evaluated, but the study of this written material will almost certainly not reveal such interesting aspects of the tender as the total throughput capability of the proposed systems or the response times or the turn-around times. These areas must be assessed by other means.

A CASE AGAINST BENCHMARKING

Ihrer (1972) concludes that Regulation E-23 is likely to force people who deal in computers to adopt extra measurement techniques, including benchmarking techniques, in addition to simulation methods, in order to comply with it. He argues that there is no substitute for simulation in the evaluation of a computer systems performance and that benchmarking is "outdated, simplistic and hopelessly inadequate." He goes on to admit that simulation is not an easy tool to use in evaluating computer system performance because it requires proficiency in its use and a fair amount of computer know-how. He does concede, however, that benchmarking can play an important role in the validation of simulation models.

The issuing of this regulation and such articles as Ihrer's in the technical press have focused attention on computer and computer system evaluation procedures. Although no obligation has been placed on anybody, these clauses have clearly highlighted the desirability, at least in the United States, for using as many techniques as are appropriate to ensure that assessments are accurate and that competition is as fair as possible.

A CASE FOR BENCHMARKING

Ihrer's article was followed in May 1973 by another article, by Goff, that put the case for benchmarking as the most accurate technique available. Goff concludes that benchmarking is the only known means of evaluating large and complex ADP systems by a common standard. He puts forward the view that the diversity of computer hardware and techniques that are used in large systems precludes their simulation by a common model. He goes further—he states that the complexity, diversity, and dynamic nature of system software also precludes their simulation by a common model. Goff suggests that for computer evaluation purposes, a benchmark is comprised of a number of elements, including:

1. A mix of job that is representative of the users' projected workload over the life of the system.
2. Demonstrations of data storage equipment and techniques.
3. Computer programs designed to test specific functions.

The problem, of course, arises in trying to establish a mix of jobs that accurately reflects the work that has to be done. Nevertheless, Goff argues, realistic programs in terms of their number, size, complexity, and input/output requirements can be established. They are then run on the vendor's premises in the presence of government examiners who can measure quantities like response times and can observe the throughput. This would be more informative than simulation because few people, apart from the manufacturer's systems programming staff, asserts Goff, really know what is going on in the simulator. Outsiders would not know what is happening in the queuing algorithms, dispatchers, spooling routines, and the rest. Further, if an accurate model was established of the total system that is being considered, then it would have to be modified regularly as the system it was intended to simulate was improved.

A MATHEMATICAL METHOD OF ASSESSMENT

Before the involvement of commerce in widespread computer use, people were passing judgments on the powers of computer configurations by mathematical means. As early as 1964 Krishnamoorthi constructed a mathematical model that described a CPU with a fixed number of channels that generated requests for computer time at random. These requests were satisfied in shared-time and so, when the number of requests exceeded the ability of the CPU to satisfy them, queues were formed. This occurred in the model as well (Krishnamoorthi & Wood, 1966).

This detailed and now classic paper assumed that both the arrival and service time distributions were exponential. Because of the data, they were not able to validate this work in practice but, as Krishnamoorthi writes, this assumption is a common one and is found in similar engineering applications.

Nielsen (1967) describes the simulation of a time-sharing system by means of a model that he uses, not as a benchmark at all, but to enable operating modes to be investigated. For example, if an organization decides that terminal users who only want moderate requests answered should get immediate service at the expense of those whose requests are more time-consuming, the management can examine this operating arrangement of an IBM 360/67 by means of the model. This work was carried out in 1966, and so, once more, it can be seen that competent simulation techniques were available for third generation computer systems nearly 10 years ago.

Another way of looking at the process of computer selection is to look at what is available for the next £10,000 or £100,000 of expenditure. Webb (May, 1972) has examined the position in the university field in the United Kingdom, and he has found that, in general, capital and operating costs appear to move in sympathy with the computing performance available, so suggesting that there are no economies of scale, at least in U.K. universities. Webb states that this is surprising because it is a widely held view that the computing power available increases as the square of the cost. This is known as *Grosch's Law*. Webb suggests that the relatively disappointing performance of large machines must be ascribed to the extent to which each computer that he has examined has to cope with a very wide range of work. He goes on to suggest that instead of following the conventional practice of buying the largest possible CPU, investment in balanced configurations would yield bigger returns—spend the next £x thousand on balancing the existing configuration.

ASSESSMENT TOOLS

The tools that are available for the assessment of computer performance include the following:

1. Simulation models.
2. Mathematical models based on operational research or more specialized mathematical techniques, like Markov models or decision theory.
3. Benchmarking using synthetic programs or typical job mixes.
4. Hardware monitors.
5. Software assessment, such as examining the operating system or using trace programs.

A Summary of Authors' Views on Benchmarking

Mr. Peter Hatt of Software Sciences Ltd. was the first to speak at the Benchmarking '74 Conference. His subject was "The role of benchmarking," and from the beginning of his lecture he left no doubt that the true role for benchmarking is as just another tool to be used for assessment purposes. He explained the process of establishing a benchmark and also the problems that this would involve, the major one being the creation of a typical job mix. Having made it clear that, even as another assessment tool, he saw benchmarking as being difficult to apply, Hatt finished by drawing attention to the advantages of contracts as a means of ensuring to both vendor and buyer that the computer system is or is not fitted for the job that has been defined for it. He suggested that, even if the contract was only a proposal or gentleman's agreement, assuming that a workload for the proposed system can be defined, a contractual approach is probably the best.

Mr. Richard Jones of Harwell was the next speaker, and his subject was "A survey of benchmarking—the state of the art." His talk spanned the full range of research and achievement in the field, from early work like Gibson Mix and PO Work Units through kernels and I/O activity to recent work using synthetic programs. Jones isolated two sources of error in applying benchmarks: the practical difficulty of running a collection of programs under controlled conditions in a complex environment and the problem of relating benchmark performance to helpful, but often inaccurate, statements about complex and varying production loads. Because he felt that these problems were difficult to surmount, Jones suggested that setting up a simple synthetic program that in its simplest form consisted of a CPU loop and an I/O loop was a better approach. In that way, he argued, the user can feed in parameters to determine how many times the program goes through or around these two loops with the result that a job is created which is as CPU- or I/O-bound as the user desires. This system can then be used to model any proposed system merely by establishing the appropriate parameters.

The first representative of a computer manufacturer to speak was **Mr. Berners-Lee** of ICL. Berners-Lee spoke in favor of benchmarking as an assessment technique. He produced slides, most of which have been reproduced in this book, to show how ICL uses benchmarking to ensure that its products are living up to their design characteristics. He developed this view by showing the delegates how, by obtaining the number of disc seeks, the number of CPU instructions in the user's program, the level of activity on the magnetic tape channels, and so on, an accurate synthetic benchmark can be established. He demonstrated a validation of this type of analytical modeling. He also made the point that all manufacturers, not only ICL, are asked to undertake gradiose benchmarks from time to time, knowing full well that they have, at best, only an outside chance of obtaining a contract. Indeed, said Berners-Lee, benchmarking on the grand scale, even if the chances of obtaining a contract look favorable, is becoming so expensive that its days are numbered. Nevertheless, he thought, a pattern of smaller, scientifically constructed benchmarks would continue to make economic sense.

After his paper, but before publication of this book, Berners-Lee sent me some later work that had been satisfactorily completed at the Atlas Laboratory, Chilton. This has been included in Appendix D.

A spokesman from another manufacturer, Univac, followed Berners-Lee. He was **Mr. Prendergast**, and he highlighted three major benchmarking areas: large time-sharing systems, the conversion area, and the application of standard software packages such as applying a data-base management package. Univac finds that they are more concerned with the second and third areas—establishing that potential users can convert readily to Univac systems and that complex software packages operate as they should on Univac computers. Prendergast confirmed Berners-Lee's view that some requests for benchmarking are almost certain not to lead to a contract even before they are attempted. He emphasized another problem manufacturers face in benchmarking, one that arose from the common expectation among some potential customers that an elaborate benchmark can be carried out in a few weeks, often with incomplete data and records. He insisted that some requests are quite unreasonable and that even when an attempt has been made to provide some sort of an answer, extra data may suddenly be produced, thus compounding a difficult situation. His solution to these problems was a simple one—manufacturers should charge potential customers for benchmarks on a time-and-materials basis so that a proper form of management control would be established, which would produce a much more professional approach for all concerned because the high costs that are incurred at the moment are passed on to the customers in one form or other, anyway.

The second day of the conference saw a series of lectures on benchmark applications in various scientific and commercial areas. The first area described was multi-access, and the speakers were **Mr. Bayly** and **Dr. Sutcliffe**, both of ICL.

Bayly spoke first. He supported a view that had already been put forward: that benchmarking is best carried out by the application of synthetic programs which emulate the work done. He agreed with previous speakers who said that difficulties of coding, data shortages, and unusual computer languages often put the approach of using existing systems at a disadvantage. Having decided that a multi-access computer system is going to be benchmarked using synthetic programs, he explained, methods must be established which examine first the number of currently active terminals and second the problems that are being tackled on them. In an attempt to provide such methods, Bayly outlined techniques for establishing an appropriate level of service to active terminals and then went on to describe the design of a script that would emulate the programs that were being processed. He announced several rules of thumb which he, among others, has found helpful in designing scripts and went on to discuss some of them in relation to response times.

Sutcliffe started by describing the experimental techniques required for applying a benchmark to a multi-access system. One technique to adopt, he said, was to avoid human terminal operators because they make mistakes, they deviate from the script, their typing is erratic, and they improve with experience. Instead, he suggested that exercisers, statistics, and a controlled environment should be used so that any output can be relied on. Having set this scene, Sutcliffe went on to describe his own simulation program, which was written in Fortran and had about 2500 statements. He showed slides, most of which are reproduced in this book, that demonstrated that response times get impossibly long after a fairly small number of users have logged on to the multi-access system. One test (see Sutcliffe's Fig. 5) indicates that a response time in the range 40–90 seconds could result from eight terminals being used at once on Algol development work. During questions, Sutcliffe outlined a range of approaches to benchmarking. The first was an analytical technique based, if possible, on performance information. In the case of future systems where performance evaluation is impossible, prediction techniques are necessary. These might include queuing theory or even simulation modeling, which could then incorporate an iterative approach. If this was then followed by a validation of the simulation against actual systems, so much the better because this could create confidence in the results.

Dr. Wichmann of the National Physical Laboratory was the next to speak, and his subject was the design of synthetic programs that could be used as benchmarks. The views he expressed were his own. Mr. Curnow of the Central Computer Agency also spoke on this subject. Wichmann started by explaining some of the mathematics involved in the work that they have carried out and then showed some slides, most of which have been reproduced, of the ability of different and named computers to cope with different workloads. He then explained how he had collected statistics from nearly 1000 Algol 60 programs at NPL and, as a check, from Oxford University as well, so that he could establish a proper, weighted mix of program statements. Armed with such a typical program, typical of all those 1,000 programs, that is, Wichmann was able to establish in practical terms an order of merit for a range of computers, and that order of merit was based on solid statistical evidence. Having produced such a chart, he went further; by picking four instructions from Algol 60 and then by examining the basic processor speed of different computers, he was able to produce a comparison of execution speeds (see Fig. 7 in Wichmann's chapter).

Curnow followed with a detailed explanation of a program that he had produced closely reflecting the standardized pattern of program statements that Wichmann had isolated. This program is listed in Appendix C. It is modular, and each module was designed to represent a genuine calculation. Each loop in the program would lead to a different result each time it was followed. He outlined some of the problems that this approach had unearthed, as well as some of its advantages. Some of the results are shown in Fig. 1 of his chapter. Another comparison that it yielded was the range of execution speeds that an IBM 360/65 and an ICL 1904A would produce when using different compilers. One application of this work, said Curnow, was in the assessment of a new machine. Such an assessment would be cumbersome, if not impossible, with the raw data that Wichmann investigated, but by refining that data and yet still maintaining the incidence of various programming instructions within statistical limits, Curnow was able to develop a package that could be readily applied to any new computer.

The first paper to cover the commercial application aspects of benchmarking was presented by **Mr. Blackman** of Arthur Andersen, a firm of chartered accountants. This application was designed for an office of a regional board of a U.K. public utility, which was primarily concerned with computerized sales and billing. The data consisted of two million commercial records, each of about 500 characters, and so was too big for daily runs. Instead, daily runs consisted of processing 1/60th of the billings with the result that all were processed every quarter of a year. This arrangement plus other work was threatening to overwhelm the existing computer, and so Arthur Andersen was called in. Because of this billing deadline, it had been decided that all new computer systems being put forward should be capable of coping with the billing load within seven hours. Blackman explained their approach to making this judgement. They broke the work into three modules, A, B, and C, and then assessed each processing path in terms of those modules. By examining the existing system from this point of view, they were able to gauge whether or not the computer systems that had been put forward would meet the seven-hour time limit.

Mr. Otway, also from Arthur Andersen, explained this assessment procedure in more detail. He covered the software necessary for the A, B, C analysis, and then he described the three computer system proposals that had been received as well as the benchmark that they were asked to run. The results are given in Table 1 of his chapter. He commented, towards the end of his lecture, that as professional consultants they were required to provide advice and not to make decisions—that part had to be left to the public utility. This meant that they examined the benchmark results as produced by each of the candidates, they judged the chances of success in other areas, like support and reliability, and, finally, they ensured as far as they could that the seven-hour time limit would not be exceeded. In all this work, said Otway, the benchmarking helped them to pass an opinion without testing the computers' capacities directly. He agreed, though, that it was not an intellectually rigorous test.

Mr. Brown from the Post Office spoke last, and, unfortunately, the recording of what he said was unsatisfactory, so only his lecture notes have been included. He began his lecture on applying benchmarks to multi-access computer systems by comparing the advantages and disadvantages of simulated and live tests, live tests being tests of systems with people operating the terminals. He concluded that as think times are so hard to simulate, live tests are preferred, and the Post Office has conducted such tests on their multi-access computer. In order to obtain a pattern of practical results, Brown explained, each user had to work to a script. All the scripts were different, and he provided details of the differences that they had incorporated in an attempt to reproduce the typical use of the various compilers. In addition, the time of the start of each script was staggered so that build-ups were prevented as far as possible. The tests were extensive and informative, but in answer to a question Brown admitted that they had been expensive— about £100,000.

I am grateful to **Mr. Kiviat**, the Technical Director of the Federal Computer Performance Evaluation and Simulation Center (FEDSIM) of the U.S. Air Force, for sending a paper on benchmarking, an edited version of which appears in Appendix E. Kiviat was a chairman of Benchmarking '74, and he also spoke after dinner at the end of the first day, at which time he made most of the points that are included in this paper. According to Kiviat, Benchmarking '74 was the first conference ever held that had been exclusively dedicated to the subject of benchmarking.

The transcripts that follow were made from tape recordings of the conference. They were printed in the U.S.A., so American spelling options have been used throughout.

Nicholas Benwell
Cranfield Institute of Technology
Bedford, U.K.   December, 1974

The Role of Benchmarking

Peter Hatt

Principal Consultant, Software Sciences Limited

We are sitting in a conference called *Benchmarking*, and right from the start I'd like to object to the name because if you read the handouts, you'll find that people are talking about all sorts of other things as well. I'm going to do exactly the same thing because benchmarking is only one of a large number of tools available to us for measuring the performance of machines and working out effectively which machine to get. So let's try and get some definitions.

What are we trying to do? Are we trying to measure machine power? The literature is full of descriptions of machine power. What is it? A lot of Post Office Work Units, Gibson Mixes based on the Atlas as a base of 100, or any of the other measures of machine power. When you go and talk to anybody in a commercial or scientific computing environment, they say things like, "We need a more powerful machine." What do they mean? Do they want more discs, do they want more core? Do they want faster core? Do they need a bigger printer, a faster printer? What is it that they mean by "a more powerful machine"? We might say, then, that one of our objectives is to try to define and measure machine power in such a way that we can compare one machine with another.

One of the objectives of the activities surrounding benchmarking might be to test the machine's ability to do a specific job. If we're thinking in terms of a process control machine, then that

1

machine has to receive signals from whatever process it's controlling and get the answers back quickly enough to stop the whole thing blowing up. If we're talking about a commercial data processing application, we might have to process umpteen million records a day and go all through those and perhaps do very little computing. So it's very necessary, I think, to compare the job we want to do with the machine we expect to do it.

What about the projection of performance? Having written the word, I'm not quite sure I like it. It's the projection forward of the growth of the work we're trying to do on the machine to the time in the future when we might have to buy a bigger machine. We want to know in advance (particularly anybody in government wants to know some years in advance) whether we're going to need a bigger machine. So we want to project the workload and see how a given machine will perform against it in the future.

Other people would define a *benchmark* as a sort of competition for manufacturers. The competition is not whether your machine is better than anybody else's, but whether you're better at doing benchmarks, as I think will be talked about later. You'll probably be told how to do it. There are many definitions, and I'm not going to attempt to say which is the right one. I'm just going to plow on and assume that all the definitions are correct in their own environment.

Let's talk about the traditional benchmark. Basically, you chuck at a number of machines a whole pile of instructions, valuable and otherwise. Each job stream, which may be defined or undefined when you start off, is bunged into the machine, and you see how long it takes to do it all. Well, there are some situations where you might think that this is probably not a bad approach. If you have an existing running system, it's doing something. If for some reason or another—either because the mice have got into the CPU, or because you want to change the software to keep up with everybody else—you decide to invest in a new system, then you can take your existing work and run it under new hardware or under new software (that is, providing you take a true sample of the day's work—whatever that may be—and run it under operational conditions, rather than having a whole lot of highly trained operators changing the discs and the tapes and running around in circles pumping the thing along with the assistance of the manufacturer's systems engineer). There's a fair chance that you will, indeed, get some sort of answer that's worth having. I do believe that there is a role for this type of benchmark on real systems like software or operating systems design.

We are all bedeviled by the vagaries of operating systems. However they've worked, it always seems to be operating systems that people understand least. (I was, for example, sitting at a terminal the day before yesterday and was suddenly switched off the machine for ten minutes. I phoned the operators and said, "What's on the computer?" and they said, "Yours is the only job." Mr. Jones is going to discuss the state of the art in the next chapter.) If you are designing new software, you need to continuously test it to see if it's getting better, and this business of just chucking instructions at it isn't a bad way of doing it.

I think it works well for the monitoring of performance, too. You have a machine which is running at a certain load, and you want to see whether you're getting the best possible performance out of it, whether you should have new hardware or add some hardware, increase the size of the core, this sort of thing, or whether you should change to some new and fantastic operating system that's really going to work. Then it is not a bad idea to try tuning the one you've got to see just what performance you're getting out. Some operating systems (far too few) actually pump out statistics of what's going on inside.

So how are we going to select this mass of instructions we're going to hurl at the system? Well, one traditional and well-used approach—and I'm in the middle of experts here who've all done it—is to take a "typical day's load." In a scientific system, what's a typical day? In a commercial system, are you going to have Wednesday when you do the payroll, or are you going to have Monday when you do the bills of material for next week, or are you going to pick the ordinary sort of typical day's load, which is yesterday's backlog? I don't know. How do you pick a typical day's load? Do you sort of preconceive what a typical day's load would be if there were ever going to be a typical day?

Or are you going to actually use the load that you put out in the proposals when you went out to buy this heap of stuff? Because one thing that happens is your plans for your machine are at point A, and the point actually reached with what you do is point B, and these are wide apart. Five years after the original proposal, your machine is doing something totally different from what you originally suggested it should do. Usually it is doing less, but sometimes it is doing a lot more. Do you just guess at it and say, "Well, every day we do 27 Fortran compilations, we do some Cobol combinations, we run the college accounts and one or two other things. Let's sort of put together a lot of our most likely programs, carefully mixed with I/O balance, put them into a job stream [preferably at random, because if you start choosing job streams you can affect the results quite considerably], and just shovel them in." Then write out your report, which says, "The machine did all this stuff in four hours; therefore, I am convinced that a bigger machine will do it in two." I don't know. I hope someone will tell us.

But here's another way. You construct programs that are carefully designed to reflect the amount of compute intensity in whatever work it is you want to run. Here we are talking of something like the Gibson Mix or Post Office Work Unit type of measurement. I'm not suggesting that either of those things is the right one—certainly, Gibson Mix doesn't appear to be the right one. You will know what the computing intensity of your normal job is. You work out what I/O intensity you're going to expect out of the machine, how many reads and writes and how many seeks, how many miles of tape it's going to absorb a day. You mix these together in suitable proportions according to any one of a number of recipes (some of these recipes I'm sure others at this conference will give you), you compile all this stuff, and you bung it at the machine according to a preconceived idea of how long it's supposed to take to run.

One has to be very careful of the "compiler effect" when you compile things. As I'm sure everybody knows, they can be op-timized, although one or two compilers actually pessimize them! Things are optimized either in terms of the speed of compiling or in terms of the speed of running the job, or in some other form, and this is all widely advertised in the material you get when you get a compiler. It does make quite a difference what happens to a syn-thetic program.

In the last year, I've worked for IBM in an office north of New York. I had a colleague sitting across the desk from me whose entire duties for that year were to write instructions for IBM systems engineers in the field on how to tune a benchmark. It was a very expensive piece of paper when it came out because the chap flew all over the world to get opinions, but I will say this—it worked. I've run benchmarks using this simple set of instructions, which says you do the following things to the job stream and you will get better results than the chap next door, unless he happens to be CDC. It doesn't seem to matter what they do to the job stream, they still seem to do it faster than anybody else.

The other thing, of course, is to fudge the beastly thing. That is, if you don't get the results you want, you alter the stuff you shovel in. In addition, tuning up the job stream is extremely im-portant, and here one actually needs to perm every program in the job stream with every other one and see what order they should go in to get them going fastest. You fiddle with the priorities a bit, too. But the programs themselves can be fudged, and I see that large contingents from the Central Computer Agency (CCA) exist just to prevent people from fudging the program they are going to use for their acceptance tests. So beware of these things.

Manufacturers can, do, and one might even contend should, tune their benchmarks. It keeps them all in business, with everyone buying bigger and bigger machines. We need more and more people like me to come and sort out the mess. So perhaps it is right that benchmarks should be tuned, because in tuning the benchmark you do learn something about what goes on in the operating system, and it's not a bad idea to have somebody who knows that, because it may help you in the future. As for measuring the power of the machine, or seeing whether it will do the job, or any of the other things I said at the beginning, I think a tuned benchmark is a complete load of rubbish.

All is not gloom. I have a solution that I think is right. There are a number of other speakers who'll be talking to you today and tomorrow who also have solutions, some of them different from each other. I imagine all of them are quite different from mine, and they are all equally convinced they're right.

What are we trying to do here? When we buy a machine, we want to make sure the manufacturer delivers something according to a fixed contract of some kind. Now the contract may be implied, as in a proposal, in that the proposal could be held to be a statement of what the manufacturer said he was going to do. It could be a sort of gentleman's agreement between the DP manager and everybody else that there is an objective in what they want to do with the machine, and they want to make sure the machine fulfills it. Or it could be one of the more complex types of contract common in defense type work, where the thing actually has to perform to some kind of specification, and we've got to write this specification. We've got to be able to say we want the machine to do X, whatever it is. Now we have to search around for a mechanism so that when we turn the thing on, and when it's all running, we know whether it is doing X or not.

What we have to do is first to estimate a workload in some way, and the workload can be a firm, main workload, that is, we want to do the work we are already doing, only twice as much of it. Alternatively, it can be a sort of envisaged workload where you say, "We are going to open a bureau, and we're going to load it up with the following work, but we still want to have capacity to do some more work, and we don't even know what that is." Or it can be somewhere in between—it can be semifirm. Somehow or other we have to establish a workload.

There is a mechanism for doing this already in existence. In the systems simulators, such as SCERT, you can define the workload in terms of how many imputs there are, how many instructions there are in the compute, and what sort of order it all runs in. We then shovel it in, and the simulator will massage this against some known or assumed characteristics of a machine and finally come out with some answers which say, "Yes, it will do this in the following time." So there is a way of defining workload.

What I would look for, and I hope one day to have an opportunity to do this, is a way of describing the workload in very much simpler terms. I believe there are only about eight possible program logics on the large scale, and to produce these logics one should be able to define a number of jobs in such a way that automatically you can produce the input to such a thing as SCERT. You can do this simply by saying, this is a payroll for 10,000 men, this is a bill of materials operation for making 100 motor cars a day, or, this is a university application, and we expect the Fortran compilations and the running characteristics to be of this type and there to be so many of them. I really believe that with the results of this activity, having to borrow the workload in broad terms and having automatically generated a definition of the workload, you can do two things. Either you can generate some synthetic programs which actually run, programs that look like the jobs you're going to do. Or you can shovel this input into a simulator.

So what do you get? You get a means of planning the hardware you want to buy anyway, you have a means of specifying in a contract what it is that you want to do, and shut up in your safe you've got the synthetic programs. When the machine arrives in a couple of years' time, you can actually put on those programs, always assuming that the manufacturer hasn't changed the programming language on the way, and you have an opportunity to accept or reject the machine. The decision will be based on what the manufacturer said he was going to do. At the same time the same sort of activity can be used for looking at new applications to see whether they'll fit onto your system, for looking at new systems to see whether they'll do more work, and for looking at actual jobs whose run costs you haven't even started to assess. I know it's all very blue sky, but this is what I think can be done, and I hope that, as I say, one day I'll have the chance to do it.

There are, however, some hazards. One I've already spoken about is this frightful compiler effect. You take compilers of two manufacturers who both claim they are optimizing in a particular way and shove the same stuff into them. You'll get different code out, it'll be optimized in different ways, and the same job will take different times to run on essentially similar machines with similar core speeds, facilities, access methods, and so on. Now this is a tremendous hazard of the synthetic program, especially if it's automatically generated. I know one of the authors, Harry Curnow, has spent ages trying to write Fortran programs that would actually be free of these curious optimization effects.

Another hazard is that the machine will run the programs that it's going to run as a benchmark, and that the job stream will fall into a happy equilibrium state, with everything just going around and around but not really proving anything. This is particularly a hazard in the testing of the multi-access type of machine.

Another hazard is a sort of faith or bias on the part of the people producing the synthetic programs or the synthetic program generator. I've been standing here for half an hour giving you an extremely biased, but I hope not cynical, view of the problems of benchmarking. I can equally have faith in or bias toward how I believe benchmarks should physically be run in any particular case. All experimentation bias on the part of the experimenter produces results way outside the range of normally statistically acceptable results you would get.

There are several ways of trying to check the machine that is going to run 100 terminals and eight remote job entry points. One way is to poke into the software of the machine as far forward as you can in the communications handlers. This is something that makes the machine think it is receiving messages or makes the software think it is receiving messages, and then to program inside the same machine the messages it's going to send itself. As with all this work, there is the danger that, as you put in the thermometer, the temperature of the bath water drops. If you can identify just what overhead is imposed by these software activities, by some more software that identifies overheads and hopefully its own as well, then there's a chance that you can get stuff out by this means. It is very, very useful for the initial testing of multi-access systems on a single thread basis, or even on a multi-threaded basis, providing you don't use it for performance projection. You will then know that if the messages do come in in much the same way as you're trying to get them in, then they will be processed and produce some results more or less as the programmer intended.

Another thing to do is to plug into the front of the machine some sort of imitation network in a hardware form, some sort of device with a lot of octopus-like cables hanging out that you plug into the communications controller of the system. In there, then, messages will be sent to the system in some sort of form very similar to the ones it's going to expect from its network in the future.

I think this is probably the route everybody's got to go. There are one or two tentative attempts to produce these things, and I'm sure people who've read much more widely than I have will know about these.

So far, I've left out one other method, and that is the trained monkey approach, where you get all the people in the room to sit at a terminal with either a script or just their imaginations, and they just keep throwing numbers at the machine. I know of Air Traffic Control Systems that have been tested in this way. I come by train whenever I can now, but I suppose the signaling system is tested that way as well! I have just left that out because I don't think that is a competent way of testing anything at all except the inventiveness of the monkeys at the end. With either of these two approaches, software or hardware, you may or may not use a message generator. If you don't use a message generator, all you're doing really is using the trained monkey approach in an automated fashion. If you sit and write out a long script, punch it up on cards, and shovel it in through this thing, you're not exercising the system. All you've done is to exercise it even less than the monkeys would because you've got only one monkey writing the stuff.

So what you really need is some sort of scripting mechanism that enables you to write, in fairly simple language, descriptions of what is supposed to go on in the network and what responses are expected from the system. The system calls out on the network descriptions of what responses it gets back and read/write calls, and all these things have to be included in your scripting language. It then generates a message stream together with some sort of random timing system, or pseudo-random timing system, that's going to feed these things in at the sort of speed that you expect the network to be able to cope with in the future.

I think, then, the real answer to the exercising and testing of the capacity of multi-access systems is going to be a hardware network simulator, or emulator, whichever is the right word, filled with a scripted message generator. I believe that this thing is coming, and someone will produce one commercially, and you'll be able to hire it. It will come in a van to plug into your computer and play networks for you. It will certainly need its own trained staff of people to actually put it together and script it.

I don't think we know nearly enough about the testing of operating systems. I think operating systems stink! There's hardly one decent one, and people who have difficult jobs usually end up by so distorting the manufacturer's operating system that they have to write one themselves. And even those stink! Somebody, somehow, has got to find a way of discovering how to check an operating system to make sure that it performs according to the beautiful brochures that come out five years before the system itself. Whether it's working in virtual machines, whether it's working on single job streams or multiple job streams, whether it's a dozen little baby computers sitting around a mother hen or one vast thing that sits there and rumbles, and whether it's blue, orange, grey, or pink, the operating system inside there has got to run that thing in such a way that you can say with confidence that if I put this sort of work in, it's going to get done in this way at that time.

You've also got to be able to know that it doesn't occasionally inject stuff into the thing, as I'm perfectly convinced the 1106 I was playing with the day before yesterday did. I think it made it up and pushed it in there. There was a job running that wasn't mine, and I was the only person on the machine. I'm not a sufficient enough software expert to even suggest how one might start benchmarking an operating system and really improve its performance. There will be people who say, "Ah, you do it with a hardware monitor." It is absolutely marvelous; it tells you everything that's going on in there, but it doesn't tell you why. You know how many I/O transfers there are, how many swap-outs there are, and all the rest of it, because you can put your probes all over the machine. Maybe hardware monitors are the answer, but personally I think they come under the sort of faith and bias end of the market that we were talking about earlier.

DISCUSSION

First Day Chairman F. J. M. Laver (former Board Member for Data Processing, The Post Office): Really, we're talking about making measurements. By implication, if you make a measurement, you make the measurement with some sort of accuracy. What sort of accuracy are we talking about?

Mr. Hatt: I have seen projected operational systems where they've been as much as 300 percent out. A job that was supposed to be done in one shift, five days a week, taking three shifts and seven days a week, and even then requiring an additional, identical machine to run it, to do the job that was originally just going to take one machine a third of a day. The error here is more than 300 percent; it's 600 percent out. I have seen people look in the air and say, "Well, that looks like a nice machine; it looks about the right size for the job. We won't make any measurements; we'll buy one and wait and see what happens." And they've been happy ever after. So I don't know with what accuracy one can measure the performance of machines. All I do know is that we had better start doing it a darn sight more accurately than we are now.

(Inaudible question)

Mr. Hatt: I think I said when talking about the SCERT-type simulator and the possibility of generating input for that sort of thing, that SCERT and its colleagues operate on recorded, known, or assumed characteristics of the machine. I think I said that. I meant to. Now then, it's possible to assume certain characteristics of a machine even while it's on the drawing board because, believe it or not (and I only know this by having worked right inside a laboratory for a computer manufacturer), computer manufacturers actually do start out to build a machine with certain characteristics. This surprised me when I discovered it, but it is true. Because of this then, they can say this machine is designed to behave in the following manner. Its I/O transfers would take so long, it can do so many operations all at the same time, and it beats as it sweeps as it cleans, and all the other things. It is possible, if you've got the money and time, to write down all these characteristics and feed them to a simulator which then enables you to simulate the thing as though it were an existing machine. Fine so far. Also, through working inside what one usually refers to as a large computer manufacturing firm, I discovered that when the machine is finally announced with a blast of trumpets or appears under veils while everyone mutters about it, it is quite different from what the manufacturer said he was going to make. It's completely different. Fine, if we can do it, but for heaven's sake, I ask the manufacturers, who are probably going to murder me this evening, if they're going to change what the machine's going to look like, for heaven's sake, tell us! Don't suddenly spring it on us when we've had the thing installed for a month. That's all.

R. Prendergast (Univac): If you think operating systems stink, and you don't know the answers, would you like to tell us who does know the answers, and who can also deliver?

Mr. Hatt: It is the manufacturers' job, if they're selling something, for heaven's sake, to make it work. This is an old argument. Is it right that the machine manufacturers should write the software, or should there be an independent software industry that writes software for hardware machines? I believe there should be an independent industry. I don't think manufacturers should be allowed to write their own software. I think every piece of coding in a manufacturer's offices and factories should be torn up and pulped. I think software should go out to people who have no interest in anything but the performance of that software. They don't have to prove anything except that they can write software to specifications.

Unidentified speaker: How can you measure the workload?

Mr. Hatt: Well, I started by describing your job in some form which can then be automatically converted into numbers of I/Os, computing intensity, the color of the job, if you like. But it should be possible to describe most jobs because most jobs have been done. Now, if we get further into process control and this sort of thing, then whoever's working on prescribing what the job is to be must also work on describing the workload, and somehow or other then we've got to convert that into programs and run them on the machine. I think this is what I said.

Unidentified speaker: We have been working for about 10 to 15 years in this business and we have a historical workload in our computers today, but the next problem is different. We never have enough historical data.

Mr. Hatt: Yes, I agree entirely. I've already tried to say this is the problem. Fortunately, because I'm speaking first on the subject of what benchmarks are for, I don't have to answer the thing. Somebody much cleverer than me follows, and he's going to tell you the solution.

Unidentified speaker (IBM): I think I should be a bit cynical about your, as it were, representation of workloads as units of, say, payrolls or bills of material. If that were possible, I'm sure that all software houses would be out of business, because once you've created a payroll, it would suit everybody.

Mr. Hatt: You're quite right.

Previous speaker: Therefore, there is no such representation; there is no method, and everybody is unique. All we can do is to try to achieve some sort of degree of accuracy in representation. If we are not being accurate, but we know where the fluctuations lie, we may be able to do a performance evaluation against a particular workload. What I think people fail to recognize is that they are not working with absolutes. They're working with figures which are meant to be representative. If some people would get out of their minds the fact that workloads can be actually represented by actually having the workload, then we will be nearer the truth, and we will be nearer actually finding a solution.

Mr. Hatt: Yes, there are two points here. One, I was perhaps being facile for the purposes of this presentation in my description of how to label workloads as being of this type of program or that type of program. What I was talking about was a mechanism for generating a representation of a workload which was easier than sitting down and writing it all out. The other thing is, nobody ever tests a workload on a computer, unless the computer is going to live in a closed process control environment, because each workload is never what you said it was going to be. It's either more or less different. It's not going to be the same, whatever you do. What you also have to do, I think, is to come back and keep calibrating your measuring instrument. If you have a thing that generates workloads and simulates computers and so forth, it's marvelous. Unless you then look at it afterwards and say that what actually happened is this, you might just as well be an economist!

Mr. Jackson (Peat Marwick & Mitchell): My comments are entirely personal. It was just to follow on from the last speaker, who said that all sorts of things can be different in all sorts of ways, so what's the use of planning, anyway? I suppose it's pertinent to say that some changes matter more than other changes, and maybe these differ from computer to computer and operating system to operating system. Is it possible, in other words, to determine what the sensitivities are, not to say this will be so, but to say certain things will change and this is the direction of changes that matters?

Mr. Hatt: I hope so; I just think there's got to be a lot more time spent on these things. I don't think enough people concern themselves, and I'll tell you why. Because in the ultimate, the cheapest way of getting more performance out of a machine is to buy a bigger or another one and add them together. It's the cheapest way. You can spend hours and hours and millions of pounds poking around with an operating system to try and increase its efficiency by 5 percent. For about a quarter of the money you can go and buy a bigger machine and try it. That isn't cynicism, that's really true. The cheapest way of getting better performance is to buy more machines and not worry about what goes in. That's why CDC machines always win all the benchmarks; they're all so enormous it doesn't matter what you shovel into them. The operating system, I think, is much the same as all the others.

A Survey of Benchmarking: The State of the Art

Richard Jones

Computer Sciences Division, Harwell

Like Mr. Hatt, I have a title which leaves plenty of scope for my imagination and so, although I feel that he said in many ways a lot of the things that I was going to say, and I suspect he said quite a lot of things that a lot of other people were going to say, I'm going to say them again, largely because the other alternative is for me to walk out after saying, "Rubbish!"

I am proposing to cover this topic in the following fashion: First of all, I want to look at the way that benchmarking has evolved over the past few years, and I want to try and look at the reasons why it has evolved in this way. I then want to say what I think the guiding principles are in benchmarking and why most benchmarks are unsatisfactory when you measure them against these criteria. I then want to discuss what I think of the most hopeful recent work and attempt to look ahead at the way I think we should be going.

Let me define a *benchmark* as a means of estimating computer performance by measuring experiments on the computer concerned. In general, I think, my remarks are going to be aimed at the general-purpose computer-center type of installation, rather than a dedicated set-up.

In the beginning, when men wanted to measure their computer's virility, they attempted to do it by comparing the speed of its central processor with other computers. The first thing they did was

15

to take typical instructions—loads, stores, and whatever computers did in those far-off days—and compare them with each other. They got a comparison, but they were fairly rapidly faced with the problem of what a typical instruction might be. So they moved on to instruction mixes, to the two famous ones called Gibson and Post Office. With these mixes you take a judicious blend of instructions, jumble them all together, stick them through the computer, and you see how long it takes for the computer to execute them. You do the same with other computers, and you say computer A is better than computer B. Amazingly, this technique still seems to be in use today; we see in the pages of no less a magazine than *Computing* within the last year, figures purporting to show how much faster the New Range Machines are than the equivalent IBM, Univac, etc. However, even in those far-off days, it obviously wasn't good enough because, again, nobody could agree on what a typical instruction mix was going to be. So they moved on to things called *kernels*.

Kernels are where you look at a program, you hack out of the program its innermost, darkest recesses where all the action is. If it's a high-level language, you compile it, and you stuff it through the computer. It has the advantage (and I think, in contrast to the previous author, this *is* an advantage) of taking into account the compiler efficiency. I think that for a dedicated machine, for example Meteorological Office installations where you've got a very large machine which is CPU bound and fairly well dedicated, this is still a reasonable approach to take. However, as computing moved away from number crunching, when these nasty commerical places started getting hold of computers, it dawned on people that what influenced a computer's performance were other things apart from the CPU speed—in particular, the I/O activity and the way that it interacted with the CPU activity. So people started to pick up single programs which they bunged into the machine to see how it went. They compared the execution times, but they then found that this wasn't good enough because there was a thing called *multiprogramming* which had come down from the gods.

This approach was insufficiently general because the performance of programs is affected by what's being executed with them and hence what's competing for the computer's resources. In addition, you can't predict the throughput from the performance of a single job. So what did people do? They slipped a little bit further down the slope, and they started to collect streams of simple jobs. They ran the job, they picked a set of jobs out of a workload, and they put them all together into a stream. The jobs tended to be "cards in–lines out" because these are nice repeatable jobs, and you don't have any nasty problems with setting the thing up. You run this through the first machine, and then you run it through the other machine, and you make a comparison.

One of the classics in this area was the Oxford Benchmark which is run on a number of machines. It's held by many to be—or it was held by many to be—a good representation of a scientific workload. I gather from the Oxford University people that it has performed valiant service, and it has correctly predicted the improved performance that you obtain from enhancements to operating systems. I must admit that we've done this sort of thing ourselves. We've picked up streams of fairly simple jobs, and it's quite a good method of predicting enhancement.

But installations no longer run exclusively cards in–lines out. You've got things like data bases, things like permanent file stores, all these things that complicate. In addition, you've got interactive computing, where you want to measure not only the throughput but the response as well. So the next stage down the slippery slope is to attempt to build a benchmark to model this. You freeze and copy your data files, you select programs to match various aspects of your workload, you get your language mix right, you get the size of the jobs right, you get the right amount of I/O, you copy all the jobs, you get them to work on the computer on which you do the benchmarking, you put everything on the file store of the new machine. Now you want to model interactive computing where you've got the difficulty of repeatability with humans and terminals, so you start to simulate terminal systems either by using a separate computer or by means of an in-core program that pushes commands into the terminal handling software, following suitable scripts simulating think-times. An example of this sort of benchmark would be Glasgow University's one of a couple of years ago, where they attempted to find out whether a 1900 series computer, with which they were about to be foisted, would have the required power. I understand that it took them something on the order of three or four man years to create their benchmark and to get the thing assembled and running.

So, what's happening? Like many others who have gone through this procedure, you are getting more and more complex; you're trying to match the growing complexity of hardware and software and programs by more and more complex benchmarking. And you're creating a monster. The whole process is so incredibly difficult—you've got the vast problem of collecting jobs, of matching the workload characteristics, of transferring it; running it's a nightmare, everything's got to be initialized, it takes an age to run, you've got to check the output and make sure everything's repeatable. If you're not careful, you're putting a lot more in than you're getting out.

If I can paraphrase an ancient Egyptian proverb that I saw applied to data base management, although I think it translates fairly accurately; "This kind of benchmarking has the appetite of an elephant but the exhaust of a constipated flea."

So in a sense this kind of benchmarking, one might say, is the state of the art, but because of the amount of effort and the expense that you've got to put into it, I can't really see that for most installations it's advisable to find a benchmark that will do. Apparently the Oxford University Benchmark took six to eight man months to collect and assemble; our one took us five or six man months I guess; you compare it with five man years and you can obviously go on further from there. What are you going to do about the networks or distributed systems? Well, I think what we've got to do is we've got to avoid this kind of complicated benchmark. So let me now sketch a few points that I think you should bear in mind when you are trying to create some kind of a test to measure what your computer can do. In addition, of course, I should point out that these are the sort of things that a lot of very competent people are already thinking about.

First of all, what on earth are you trying to achieve and, while we're at it, why on earth do you want this new computer or this new enhancement or whatever it is, anyway? Even more important, does the organization want it? Or is demand being generated from within the computer center itself? These are important questions that I think you've got to ask yourself right at the very beginning because I think they will influence very strongly the kind of benchmark that you're going to do. You know, why do you want to quantify the improvement that you're presumably expecting? Do you want a directionality, just to say, "It's going to improve," or do you want to say, "I'm going to get 50 percent improvement on throughput"? Is it feasible or sensible or possible to measure in a meaningful way what it is that you want to measure? Do you want to look at the whole system performance applied to the whole workload or would a subset do? Is all you really need to find out that the compilers compile code in a reasonable kind of way? So, the thing is, you must plan the experiments that you're going to do very carefully. Secondly, you must be aware that the workload for a general computer center is very variable. If this is what you want to model, you are going to need to do a series of runs, to see how the computer can deal with the varying workload. You should surely set parameters to vary and set up a group of runs to try to measure the effects of this variation.

In this area I think I should refer you to articles in a book called *Statistical computer performance evaluation* (Freiberger, 1972), where the author describes how such experiments can be set up and discusses the statistical techniques that you need in order to evaluate them. In addition, I'd like to refer you to an article by Hughes (1974) on computer performance evaluation.

The other thing that you must be aware of is the variability that can occur on even apparently identical runs. I can refer you to an article by Thomas Bell of The Rand Corporation (1971-1973) in the proceedings of SHARE where he lists some of the assumptions that everybody takes for granted, but that he says, and I'm bound to believe him, are not true. For example, "The elapsed time to execute a section of program has zero variance. If several passes are made through this same section, without terminating the program, the elapsed time will be constant." It seems an obvious thing, but it may very well not be true. Secondly, "The elapsed time for independent execution for the same program has zero variance. Minor changes in allocating files, positioning in memory and exact starting times don't change the elapsed time." So that even if you are repeating the same test on the same computer, you may not get the same results. You must think about how you are going to monitor the performance. Is it sufficient to take the clock-on-the-wall time as the elapsed time from the start to the finish? Or how about plotting graphs of the information that you get logged, end-of-job- times, times of end of steps. If there's an accounting system working, and if you get the cost of each job given, then plot the accumulated value of the jobs run against time. Third, use software monitors or hardware monitors to find the utilization of the system components, find out where the bottlenecks are, and then find out why they are where they are.

Then think about where you're going to put the effort. Try to put the effort into designing these tests, into monitoring and measuring. Don't spend all your time collecting jobs and getting them to run on unfamiliar machines. It all boils down to that old expression, *good experimental technique*. You are running an experiment. First, you face the practical difficulty, the running of a collection of programs under controlled conditions in a complex environment, and then the more fundamental difficulty of relating benchmark performance to meaningful statements about complex varying production loads. The onus is inevitably on the user, both to formulate a testable proposition and to ensure experimental rigor in carrying out the test. The value of the test will depend on how precisely the relationship between benchmark and production can be established.

So, on all these points, just to hammer the point home, I think that the very complicated benchmark is liable to fall down. The complication of its creation diverts you from thinking about what your objectives are. The complication of running it makes it impossible to be flexible. The expense of running it makes it difficult to repeat the experiments. The collection of jobs, the setting up, it all takes time. So I don't think the very complicated benchmark, when applied to real jobs to measure throughput and overall system performance, has got a future.

So where are we going to go? Or where are some people going, if benchmarking's not going to become just the placebo for the management because management likes to have a figure, one figure which they can use as a criterion of excellence for your computer installation: the number of jobs through or so many hours CPU time and so on? How then are we going to get something valuable, how do some people get something valuable out of bench-marking? It's an important question and although, like the last author, I am a cynic about benchmarks, I think that they have got a place; I'm certain they've got a place because ultimately there can be no other criterion except actually running stuff on the machine concerned. Well, I think that the way ahead lies in the use of the synthetic jobs that Mr. Hatt mentioned. Again, this is going to be discussed further, so I don't particularly want to steal anybody's thunder.

Let me just give you yet another introduction into synthetic jobs. By *synthetic job* I mean a program that is written to exercise a computer's resources in a way that you can vary by means of a few input parameters. So, in its simplest form, the synthetic job could be the CPU loop and an I/O loop. You feed in parameters to determine how many times you go through or round these two loops. In that way you can create a job that is as CPU bound or as I/O bound as you like. You duplicate this job, giving it various parameters, and you build up a job stream, which you can use to match any desired profile that you like. And this technique gives us a very flexible tool that can be readily made to run on any computer. It leaves the experimenter free to concentrate on the experiments that he wants to do. It's been quoted in a number of recent articles and quoted already at this conference. It's going to be quoted again. I think it's a concept which is catching on.

In our installation we've used a very simple version which, basically, consisted only of a CPU loop and an I/O loop, and we certainly found it very valuable for testing enhancements when you improve on the same system, i.e., for eventually comparing the system with itself. You can use a very simple-minded synthetic job to give you some kind of a feel, at least a directionality and possibly in more exact terms, as to what you're getting out of any enhancement that you're trying to do. However, before we can exploit this, we must understand more about the character of workload; we must find it out in terms of the function of the work, rather than of the computer on which we're going to try to run this work. For example, a trivial example, if we say that the state of an installation workload is processor bound, that is a statement about the computer as well as about the workload because all we're saying is that that's the limiting resource, so we've got to burrow in. Again like the previous author, I believe that there are a few critical characteristics that you're going to be able to dig out to characterize a workload. Using these few criteria, you create synthetic jobs to build up streams of jobs which you can then run, after suitable validation, which I think has to be added. If we want to do models or run experiments to model complex workloads, this is the way we're going to have to do it.

However, a word of warning from Hughes again (1974) just to back up what I was saying. In synthetic programs, the resource requirements are decoupled as far as possible so that you can make them very flexible and very easy to work with. However, their use requires a degree of understanding of the workload to match the greater degree of control that one has. While it's easy to make them superficially portable, synthetic programs require careful validation against real programs for every system to which they'll be applied. So I believe that this is the way ahead, but I believe that we're not there yet. The state of the art has a long way to go before we can have a lot of confidence in the results of benchmarking to obtain system performance figures. So it's not safe to rely on a single benchmark as the sole method of assessing the potential of a computer system.

There are other techniques of modeling computer performance, namely the Monte Carlo simulation type of program or the analytical model type of program. These are cheaper to run repeatedly, and so you could use them to suggest further experiments that you might like to try to verify your simulation. It's felt, however, that these techniques are not very reliable in this area either. An article in Freiberger's book (1972) queries the validity of a number of common assumptions made, particularly with regard to the demand mechanism that one has within simulation models.

For a typical example of this work, I would like to describe a method used by one U.S. government agency for choosing a new computer. The agency officials wrote to all the manufacturers and said: this is our workload, give us a configuration. When all the configurations came in, they used the description of the configuration and the general workload figure that they supplied, and they fed them into this magic program called SCERT. This they used for the first screening mechanism, and they used it to try to get a ballpark estimate of the computer's capability. They slung out all those manufacturers whose configurations just didn't come up to scratch, and they sent the rest a short benchmark of 12 jobs, which were intended to cover all the facilities rather than to be representative. They also sent the selected manufacturers very stringent rules about running (apropos of the computer manufacturers' supposedly fiddling benchmarks) from the point of view of how many operators there could be around, whether they could premount tapes, etc. I heard a rumor that they'd asked them to levitate the machine to make sure there wasn't another machine in the background actually doing the work! Then they listed the throughput figures for these and compared them with the simulation results, and the very interesting thing was that although the relative power of the computers concerned turned out to be very different, both the simulation and this short, simple benchmark put all the computers in the same order. In addition, they were interested in interactive testing, so they asked the manufacturers to carry out a series of exercises and send them back the output and timing. They didn't send the manufacturers a script. They said, "We want to do the following things: we want to create a file, we want to edit it, we want to compile it, link it, etc.," so they just gave out a set of instructions to each manufacturer and asked them to carry them out. In addition, they sent a questionnaire to their users requesting their views on the current system and their views of what their future requirements were going to be. Finally, they took all this information, and they used a grading system as a means of selection. They had 20 criteria, which were independently judged by five assessors, and they then allocated each system marks for each criterion on the basis of the information that they had. I'm bound to say that I think that in terms of the current state of the art, this is the way that you're going to get the best feel for what a computer's likely to be able to do for you. They were not only looking at how fast the computer could do something, but they were also looking at what facilities were available, at how it looked to the users, and so on, rather than taking the sheer-brute-force approach where you set up a complicated benchmark and you fire it through the machine and it's a go/no-go system. If you are interested in benchmarking as a tool for computer selection, you've got to give the manufacturer a whole series of hoops to jump through.

Now, another point that I'd like to draw out from what I've said so far is that I think that benchmarks are of most use when you're upgrading or enhancing a particular system, where the operating system essentially stays constant and where the hardware is very nearly constant. This has been our experience; it's certainly been the experience, as I said, of the Oxford University people. Even with comparatively simple benchmarks, just using them as a tool to make sure that you're going the right way gives you a surprising amount of accuracy. Clearly, one reason for this is that you probably understand more about the system to start with, and you will know where its weak spots are. You can then design tests to see if the weak spots are still there in the new machine or whether the weak spots have moved somewhere else. You've got a lot more information to start with. In addition, it's much easier to get the jobs to run on a system that is at least similar to the one you've got. Secondly, if you're changing horses, if you're changing from one manufacturer to another or if you are moving from one range of computers to another range of computers but staying with the same manufacturer, you're likely to be altering drastically the way a computer looks to a user. You're going to find very quickly that the users are going to change their working habits in response to this. People will optimize on the system; if there's a facility there, people are going to use it.

To summarize, I hope that I've indicated that the path of ever-increasing complexity is a very dangerous one to follow. I hope that I've indicated that successful benchmarks are run as experiments with good scientific techniques—whatever that means—and that people have been doing experiments in other areas for a very long time within physics and all sorts of other sciences. There's no reason why we can't use a lot of these techniques, a lot of the statistical methods and so on, to get something more out of running experiments. Further, I think that the useful tool for benchmarking is a synthetic job, but before we can exploit it fully we've got to understand the workload, we've got to be able to characterize it in a computer-independent fashion, and until that great day dawns, we'd better hedge our bets and run as wide a set of tests as we can to see how the different methods rate the system that we're concerned with. Finally, let me emphasize this important point: if you change the environment, there is likely to be a very strong feedback mechanism on the users' habits and therefore on the users' workload.

DISCUSSION

Mr. Hatt: You said to establish exactly what you want your new computer for, a bigger or better operating system or computer. It's perfectly obvious that's so you can test the benchmark.

Mr. Jones: I don't actually know anyone who's had to buy a larger computer system so that he could just sort of fix up a benchmark for buying the next computer system, but I'm sure somebody will do it one day.

Unidentified speaker: One side of the equation is demand, and the other side is satisfaction; the satisfaction part can vary very considerably. Some manufacturer might propose a real memory system, another one might propose virtual memory, another one a paged memory, and let's say another one an associative memory system. Now how do you balance them?

Mr. Jones: Well, this is the reason why I was saying that it's important for you to characterize your workload in a way that's independent of the computer, so I take your point entirely. Surely you are going to try to create a synthetic job which has got to be a fairly sophisticated beast. Take us, as an example. We were going to use a CPU loop and an I/O loop as a synthetic program to test out a virtual storage system. We thought about this for a week, and then it suddenly dawned on us that if you tried to test a virtual storage system in this way the machine would gratefully page out everything except the tiny little bit of code that was actually active, thus making the virtual system always look superb.

What I'm meaning by a *synthetic job*, therefore, is a job that produces the sort of activity that programs do—programming characteristics such as the random search of arrays, the sequential search through arrays, I/O of various sorts, and file access in various kinds of random patterns. I don't think that there are that many parameters that you would need to treat.

Unidentified speaker: You are postulating a synthetic job; this is usually done by a manufacturer postulating a synthetic computer because he runs your benchmark on an existing machine and then scales the whole thing up to allow for the new range or future series or whatever. At what stage does the process break down, please?

Mr. Jones: Probably fairly rapidly. You've got to get your benchmark run on a system that looks as much like the system that you think you're going to buy as possible. I think that if you're in an advanced stage of abstraction, you're going to be much better off to attempt some kind of a simulation, and I think that if you haven't got the machine available, there is only one thing you can do, and that is to attempt to simulate it. You can either attempt to simulate it yourself, or you can take somebody else's word for the simulation, or you can accept the manufacturer's word.

Previous speaker: That's an unhealthy process, surely.

Mr. Jones: Well yes, quite, but again it's coming down to this thing: What is it that you want the computer that you're going to buy to do? I think it would be an unhappy process if you do take the manufacturer's word for it, but as long as you get some kind of a ballpark figure for what the system can do for you, it doesn't matter if you're 25 percent out.

Previous speaker: I think that 25 percent is rather a long way out.

Mr. Jones: It depends whether you're buying a computer for ten years or for only a year.

I should like to take that point up. How many people in this room have got computers that they had ten years ago? This is again a fact.

F. J. M. Laver (Session chairman): They're probably the wisest ones here! I think there is a real problem emerging. I begin to get the feeling that many people are really looking around for some magic box that will somehow or other measure the performance of a system they're going to buy. Or it will somehow or other measure the change in performance of a system that they've already got. They're always looking for this because, at the moment, they find they have to do it subjectively, to a large extent. They may get fed a lot of information from software monitors, hardware monitors, and benchmarks, but in the end they have to make a subjective decision. I always rather feel at the moment that they are scared of making that subjective decision because it is true that in many systems if you are 15, 20, 25 percent out in your initial estimates and there's any sort of variable workload, it will be within the capabilities of the system anyway. In addition, the software changes, new software is developed, so it's going to cost you a lot more than that in increments and hardware costs anyway. I think one's really got to be prepared to look, not just at the computer system or even just at the CPU or the I/O traffic in the system, but at the computer in its total environment. It's too easy to slip down and worry about CPU boundness and I/O traffic and so on. That's a very personal and cynical point of view, but there we are.

Unidentified speaker: I feel that you're putting the cart before the horse because in fact, in my experience, most of the subjective decisions have already been made before the benchmarking starts. Benchmarking is usually invoked either because one or another of the manufacturers feels he is getting a raw deal and puts it to higher management that they should have a benchmark to set it once and for all, or because you need the benchmark, again, to blind higher management with science.

Mr. Laver: I think you're probably right. It works both ways. I suspect it depends on which sort of organization you're working in, government or industry, and whether you are on the manufacturer's side or on the other side of the fence. However, I don't want to muddy up the issue, and there is a very important point behind all this: we've got really to discover what it is we are trying to measure. I don't think we know. It's the same with operating systems. I go further than Mr. Hatt. I'm not saying that people don't know how to design them. I go further. I would say that there are very few people around, and I have my doubts whether there are really any, who understand what an operating system is or should be.

There are two areas here. We seem to be talking about measuring all sorts of different things; we're measuring systems at the detailed levels, measuring changes in operating systems, changes in configuration. We're looking for global figures across very wide complex areas that will enable us to choose between manufacturer A's system and manufacturer B's system. We seem to be asking for one tool to do all this. Is that the right way to go about it?

Mr. Jones: We're dealing with a multi-variant function, and it's not reasonable to expect that you're going to get one number out of that function. Also, I think that part of the problem we find ourselves in is that computing is still very much at the cottage industry stage. That is, if anybody wants to do something, they go off and they do it, and they reinvent the wheel. Why? Because if they take somebody else's thing, it doesn't do exactly what they want it to do. I think that until we start to standardize programs much more than we're doing at the moment and take things much more off a sort of production line, as we do for compilers, we are going to need benchmarking.

If we need benchmarking, then for complicated jobs we need complicated benchmarking, which may be worthwhile. It is probably worth the CCA's while to go in for immensely expensive benchmarks because they're in a position to feed this information to a wide range of installations. So what we should be doing is, rather than doing one-off benchmarking, what we're really looking for is a *Which?* for computers. That is, we, the users, get together and finance, possibly through one of these magic software houses, an ongoing scheme for computer measurement and for computer comparisons. You can then pick up off the shelf a benchmark that in some way resembles your installation, and you can use it, and it's not relying on the manufacturer's benchmark at all. Clearly there is a conflict of interest, although I would be unhappy if this conference degenerated into a manufacturers-slamming competition, much as I enjoy joining in myself. I'm hoping that we can get something more positive out of this.

(Inaudible question)

Mr. Jones: That's precisely the point I'm making, that it's still a cottage industry. But I think it's going to change from that because software is getting more expensive. We are all being driven more and more, whether we like it or not, to standard packages. Unfortunately, the state of the art in standard packages is such that most standard packages are just not good enough.

Unidentified speaker: Can we really come back to this point of motivation and benchmarks because I think we've got a problem between, on the one hand, the desire for knowledge for knowledge's sake, establishing an absolute, and, on the other hand, the mucky, commercial, dirty end of the business which, I think, if we were to divide this room in two, we'd probably find half of us sitting on one side of the line and half of us sitting on the other.

Obviously, that's provable, but it's really beside the point. The thing that I think we need to establish quite clearly in questioning the whole basis of whether benchmarking is necessary or desirable and whether it's necessary in some circumstances and desirable in some circumstances, is this question of motivation. Very few of us are in a position where we can afford the luxury of knowledge for knowledge's sake, and any benchmarking system where there is a *Which?* tailor-made system, or whether we're really just trying to plan it into a scientific discipline, does depend upon our very own specific needs. These needs differ very widely, and really I think we've got to get this clear before we can even start saying, well that's a useful package, or that isn't a useful package, that's an appropriate method, or that isn't an appropriate method. It's something I'm chucking out perhaps for you to throw back at me.

Mr. Jones: Well, it's true, I think, that people should not go into benchmarking lightly. Again, at the risk of repeating myself, I think that you cannot afford not to do some kind of validation measurement. I take your point that installations feel that they have unique problems, a unique requirement. This reflects, I think, the state of the art of computing as a whole.

Let me ask you a question, then, about the way one installation feels that it's needs are different from any other. Say you take two car manufacturing companies. I don't really see that their requirements are that different one from the other. The way that they may set about tackling them and, historically, the way that their suites of computer programs have been built up, has made them feel that they are different. Their objectives, though, as companies, are substantially the same, and therefore I don't really see that the objectives of the computer group should be that different. They are running the same kind of programs, even though the programs may perform differently.

Previous speaker: I agree entirely. I think this really illustrates the point that whatever scale you look at the problem on, whether we're looking at a very small commercial user with a very small commercial machine, or whether we're looking at a large multinational corporation, or a government institution, if you try to compare the like with like, the problems are more or less the same. The answers to those problems are much the same, too, so if we take, say, a small commercial installation and try to decide whether it should buy a System 3 or a Honeywell 58 or something like that—this gives the very bottom end of the scale—their problems are exactly the same as a large government department. The motives behind doing a benchmark, to try to compare this machine with that machine, to say that it's better in these circumstances, the results are always going to be very marginal, I would suggest, even if we remove the subjective element, which we can't, because the subjective elements are part of the picture anyway. People have got to work the machines, and my preference for that sort of machine, my preference for working with those people that support that machine and provide the assistance that I get from the manufacturer, are the sort of factors that have got to be taken into account. You can never reduce it to an absolute whereby you can simply measure power. Power in this sense is meaningless shorthand, almost.

Mr. Jones: Yes, I think that particularly on the simpler side of systems, it would be surprising if you did get very different results, simply because manufacturers are aware of what other manufacturers are up to. It may be that when you get up to the giant machines, where one manufacturer essentially collars the market, then, of course, you have another situation. There's no problem then; you either take that or you take nothing. If you're comparing two machines, it is surely more important that it's got the facilities that you must have. Its speed, by comparison, is much less important. We're in a problem, because if we ignore performance measurements altogether, I feel that most people will think the manufacturer is leading them by the nose. As we've heard from the last author, the manufacturer has people who sit there working out how they can optimize their system to do this particular test in a superb way.

Unidentified speaker: I think you've got to examine the motivation for doing the thing in the first place. Only then can you get any performance measurement in its true context, to decide what value it has, because it doesn't have an absolute value on its own.

Mr. Jones: Right. A man after my own heart.

Alan Buttle (Exeter University): A question on your synthetic job steps. It strikes me that they are more a measure of the potential performance of a machine than the actual response to a user's requirement. I may have misunderstood your definition of the things but, as far as I can see, they're sort of disc exercises and CPU exercises and everything just measuring the potential in each field. In reality you've got bursts of particular kinds of activity as the jobs go through the system, so possibly what you're measuring is more how the user should mix his jobs and so on, how the work should be scheduled. Would you comment on that?

Mr. Jones: Well, first of all, the example that I quoted, of doing the simplest possible synthetic job, certainly is not the state of the art of synthetic job making. I have much more in mind: some kind of a mixture of high-level instructions with which, by means of parameters, you can determine the sort of instructions you are executing. If you like, it's rather like a very high level Gibson Mix. It's again the thing we were saying about how a user should work. This, of course, is what's going to happen. In a university, if you give a good turn around to users for some particular kind of job, then everybody's doing it. You know that if a moon landing program becomes available everybody rushes in and plays with it during his lunch hour and so clogs up the system. In any situation, if something is possible, people will start to use it so that, to answer your question, no, I don't think that a synthetic job is merely to exercise the I/Os, or to exercise the CPU, but it does that as well. The way that it is going to do it is, hopefully, going to be much more indicative of the way that people will program. Secondly, as I said, of course, the way users react to the system is important because that is a very powerful feedback mechanism.

Unidentified speaker: Do you feel that the use of synthetic jobs is the right road to be following? Really, it's like the industry and the package, or tailor-made, job written by the user. Is a synthetic job the answer to the problem, or is it better to test existing jobs with real data against various systems and determine which is going to suit you best?

Mr. Jones: I think, first of all, there is no real answer. Secondly, I think that before you embark on using synthetic jobs you would have to compare their performance very carefully against the jobs within your installation that they were purporting to simulate. I don't think that we are in the position where we can rely on synthetic jobs, because I don't think we understand enough about the workload to do it. Synthetic jobs are very useful at the moment in the current state of knowledge. Synthetic jobs are very useful for comparing the system with itself because they're easy to run, and you don't want to put a lot of effort into it. So, no, I don't necessarily think that synthetic jobs are *the* way to go, but I think they are *a* way to go, and as far as I'm concerned they look to me to be the most hopeful way to go when you're benchmarking a batch environment.

Unidentified speaker: If you didn't use the word *synthetic*, you would get over the problem. If you were to say it is a *simulated* job, it would be much better. What we're trying to do is to put parameters into a job so that they exhibit the characteristics of that job.

Mr. Jones: Yes, like everything else, we're hide-bound. The word came out of a paper by Buchholz in the *IBM System Journal* (1969), I think, and we've been lumbered with it ever since.

Two Major Manufacturers' Attitudes towards Benchmarking–I

C. M. Berners-Lee

Chief Technical Officer, Design and Planning Division
ICL Systems

I have been asked to speak on a major manufacturer's attitude to benchmarks. Before I do this, I should like to emphasize that I've consulted a number of my colleagues on this question, and what I say I think does represent an agreed consensus. What strikes me about this consensus is that it also lines up very closely with what has already been said at this conference.

As manufacturers, we are in business, and like most businessmen we take the view that business consists of the construction of mutually profitable situations. If a manufacturer gets himself into a situation in which he deceives his customer, that is extremely bad for business. It can also happen, and I regret to say it does happen, that we get into situations in which customers deceive the manufacturer. Sometimes, I'm sorry to say, it does happen, and it's a complaint I've been asked to make with, I think, very good reason. Manufacturers are sometimes put to enormous trouble over benchmarks by people in a customer organization who have no intention of doing serious business with that manufacturer. Now this happens to all manufacturers, but, because of the nature of commercial benchmarking contests, the manufacturer is bound to put his best foot forward. If the benchmark is run on his premises, of course it is run by a highly skilled benchmarking team who do, of course, tune the system for that benchmark to the utmost. Now they usually have a limited amount of time to do this, so they keep a very skilled team of people for this job, and it's just as well that everybody should understand that that is the case. We do, at ICL Systems, and I have the greatest respect for the IBM benchmarking team as well.

Now, having said that, I should go on to say that, looking at the manufacturing operation from the point of view of the design of products for the future and from the point of view of marketing products for the future, we are extremely interested in benchmarks. Benchmarks are an indication of what the market is trying to say to us. This business of providing products that are actually the things that are needed in the computer business is an extremely difficult, complex, and unsatisfactory process in many ways. Any form of feedback is extremely important—benchmarks are such a form of feedback. Now we make quite a lot of use of the information that we derive from benchmarks, and what we like to do is to measure these benchmarks thoroughly. What one really wants to get hold of is this kind of data. One wants to be able to say, for a particular class of work, that, typically, an installation of a particular type will be operating at a certain number of CPU instructions per second. Then one wants to know how many kilocharacters or kilobytes of data per second are going through EDS channels and through magnetic tape channels. One can then start thinking about the computing intensities—instructions per byte—that these different classes of business give rise to. When one starts looking at it like that, it soon becomes clear that actually the industrial classification is not very important.

I would disagree with Mr. Jones; the actual way in which data processing is done in the business does not depend very much on the industry in which the business is being conducted, but on the way that business is organized within the industry; whether it is vertically integrated or horizontally integrated, whether it's going through a centralization phase or decentralization phase, and so on.

Now, when we've got these traffic mixes, one of the things we can do, and one of the things we are most concerned to do, is to discover how our products—our present products or our projected future products—will deal with these mixes. That drives us straight into the system modeling business. Various models can be used, mostly derived from queuing considerations. One model, which we've been using for a little while, is called the football model. The idea is that the program is being kicked around inside a system, and the system behaves rather like several children who are kicking around several footballs. The number of footballs represents the level of multi-processing, and the model tells you about how the throughput on the system as a whole and the loading on each of the components increases as you raise the level of multi-processing.

Well, I've mentioned this experience to you because it tends to throw some light on this business of benchmarking, and we think that it reinforces some views that have been expressed earlier, particularly from Mr. Jones, about the way in which benchmarking is likely to evolve. When you consider all the possible factors that might affect what the elapsed time of a given real workload is going to be, you can write down a very long list:

Hardware factors

CPU speed in instructions per second
Logic speed
Memory access speed
Slave store hit rates
Store access path loading
Interrupt handling facilities
Store organization
Drum address organization
Drum channel loading
Disc rotational latency
Disc seek times
Disc channel loading
Controller loadings
Magnetic tape channel loadings
Card reader speeds
Line printer speeds
Communications processor loading
Multi-processors

Software factors

Slave store algorithms
Virtual store management algorithms
Backing store management algorithms
Scheduling algorithms
Compiling algorithms
Editing procedures
Interrupt handling
Physical file handling
Logical record management
Multiple buffering
Indexing methods

What I think we're coming to see now very clearly from modeling work and from the examination of the data that is available from system monitoring files is this: If you know all the things shown in the list, then the actual elapsed time to do those things on a given system at a given level of concurrency is constrained within very narrow limits. The number of CPU instructions in the user program and in the operating system can be divided into three: first, the number of drum accesses and the number and extent of disc seeks; second, the number of kilobytes through drum, discs, and magnetic tape channels; and third, the level of concurrency. The best way to define the *level of concurrency* is to say that it's the sum of the length of the queues in the system. What that actually means is that it's the level of multi-programming that the user sees, together with the number of slots taken up in the time sharer in the executive part of the operating system, plus an additional allowance for multi-buffering programs. Double buffering programs, for instance, count as two processes effectively, plus the fact that the operating system itself keeps giving a certain amount of additional concurrency, which can amount to about half as much again. This is because it's got a little private programming system of its own, whose processes behave like additional multi-processing programs that are being time-shared with the user programs. Well, our contention is, if you know all these factors you can predict how long it's going to take to run the work. Now, of course, in order to know these things you have got to know about the efficiency of compilers, and if you're mapping a workload from some system on which it's been measured onto some other system, then you have got to be able to fix a rate of exchange for the number of instructions. That's going to bog you, for instance, in the study of compilers and, more important, in studying the efficiency with which typical operating system functions are executed.

Well, having arrived at that conclusion, which I think is a very important conclusion, the immediate consequence of that for benchmarking is this: It points in the direction already pointed to by the last author because, you see, it doesn't actually matter what the fine details of the benchmark consist of, provided it loads the system in the same way as the real workload. Therefore, if you construct synthetic benchmarks that may have a very simple character, you can load the system in exactly the same way as all the real work. In order to do that and get it right, what you've got to do is to measure your real workload. You can do this with software, the software provided in the operating systems. Having done that, carried out the operational process, you can set up your synthetic benchmarks. That is one way. If you do that, it is very likely that you are going to find yourself doing something else because if you take all those measurements of your real work, you can also use one of the analytical modeling techniques, like the one I've just referred to, or others referred to earlier. If you do that, you are very likely to gain confidence in the use of these analytical modeling techniques. You're going to find that they're very flexible, and you can very easily examine the consequences because different changes in the configuration test some of the manufacturer's statements, and that kind of thing. This experience will make you much more circumspect about getting involved in mammoth benchmarking exercises, and it will tend to focus your attention upon certain areas that you wish to benchmark. Some of those areas are concerned with this problem of the conversion factors that you are going to use.

Now, together with an indication of what can be done with analytical modeling techniques, one of the things that I feel sure will interest you is that very early on in the validation of the particular modeling technique we use, we heard about some people in the University of Trondheim who have a Univac installation. They applied this football model to predicting the effect on that installation of increasing the amount of core. This is normally quite a difficult thing to predict. What they did was to run their benchmark and measure the loadings on the devices, the CPU, the exchangeable and fixed discs, and the mag tape, and then from that to estimate from the model the level of multi-processing that would be required to explain that throughput at those loadings. They then argued that increasing the core would increase the level of multi-processing in proportion to the free core, and then they did the sums again. They ran the benchmark again, and the comparison between the model prediction, the increase in throughput, and the actual measured values is shown in Table 1.

An important part of the model theory is a statement that as you increase the level of multi-processing, unless thrashing ensues, all the components' busyness increases in the same proportion together, and you can see in Table 1 that these measurements bear out this assertion; these ratios are very nearly constant in the two situations. That's one way in which one can validate this type of analytical modeling, which helps us to increase our understanding of the performance.

Here's another example (Table 2). In this case, of course, the accuracy you get from any analytical modeling technique, like any other modeling technique, depends on how much of the relevant data you are able to get hold of. Quite often one isn't able to get

TABLE 1   Expansion of core-store

(a) Device utilization with 128 K words of core.

	CPU	FH432	FH880	FASTRAND	MAG. TAPE
BENCHMARK	0.59	0.26	0.26	0.56	0.25

(b) Device utilizations with 192 K words of core.

	CPU	FH432	FH880	FASTRAND	MAG. TAPE
MODEL	0.79	0.35	0.35	0.75	0.33
BENCHMARK	0.77	0.39	0.38	0.74	0.35

(c) Device utilizations normalized with respect to the CPU to compare relative device loads in the two benchmark tests.

	CPU	FH432	FH880	FASTRAND	MAG. TAPE
128 K words	1.00	0.44	0.44	0.95	0.42
192 K words	1.00	0.51	0.49	0.96	0.45

Source: *A structural approach to computer performance analysis.* AFIPS Conference Proceedings 42, 1973.

hold of measurements on all the relevant devices; for instance, the mag tape loading is often missing. But if you do modeling work on just the most heavily loaded component, you can get quite accurate results, and some examples of that are shown in Table 2. This is the

TABLE 2   Benchmark measurements and model predictions
            ("Oxford" Benchmark)

	Calibration run	Run 1	Run 2	Run 3
Processor	1906A	1904A	1906A	1906A
Fast drums	1	1	2	2
Slow drums	1	1	1	—
Store (K words)	128	128	256	128
Elapsed time—actual	77	135	38	55
Elapsed time—predicted (mins)	—	137	43	66

Note: Calibration run measures the multi-processing level required to explain the observed throughput. For the other runs, this level is assumed to be proportioned to core size. Seek times are assumed to be one fifth of the nominal average.

famous Oxford Benchmark, which has been mentioned before. I used one of the runs as a calibration run to estimate the level of multi-processing for the workload as a whole. In the case where more core was added, I stepped that up to double because I felt that that situation was a George 3 type operating system. The level of multi-processing is approximately proportional to the total core usage because of the multi-processing going on within the operating system itself. As you can see in Table 2, the predicted times certainly give a pretty good qualitative indication of the change, and quantitatively it's not bad either.

It forecasts very accurately the effect of the very big change in the core that is available on the installation. What can also be done with these analytic techniques is to process system monitoring files so that you can get an ongoing validation of the technique used on your existing system.

I'm indebted to the Science Research Council for the results shown in Fig. 1. They were run on the 1906 A at the Atlas Laboratory, Chilton. Here we've got a program that plots the results from the system performance file. In this particular case the timing is eight minutes. There are 8-minute intervals across the page, and the periods are each 2 hours 40 minutes long. What is plotted here is the loadings on the various devices of the system. The top line is the total CPU utilization; the heavy line is the user program. The CPU utilization has been adjusted to include the executive time, which is not on the monitoring file, by assuming a thousand instructions per transfer, and that is added on the total fast store. Transfers per second (A) is 10, (B) is 11, and so on, and the numbers of transfers on each device are given.

I am particularly interested in this installation because it's a Paged 1906 A, and one of the things I was very interested in is whether or not it exhibits any very different pattern in the number of transfers on the swap file compared with an unpaged installation. The answer is that it doesn't exhibit any very great difference. In other words, virtual-store machines load the system in much the same way as nonvirtual-store machines. Now, having got the loadings, one can then calculate the service times on individual devices and, in this case, we used the number of core images to estimate the level of multi-processing. It's not a perfect measure by any means because of the problem of jobs which have stopped running.

The heavy line shows the analytic model's prediction of how long it would take that to process that traffic expressed as a fraction. The proportion of 1.0s is quite high. *1.0* actually means lying between .95 and 1.05, *1.1* between 1.05 and 1.15, and so on. It's

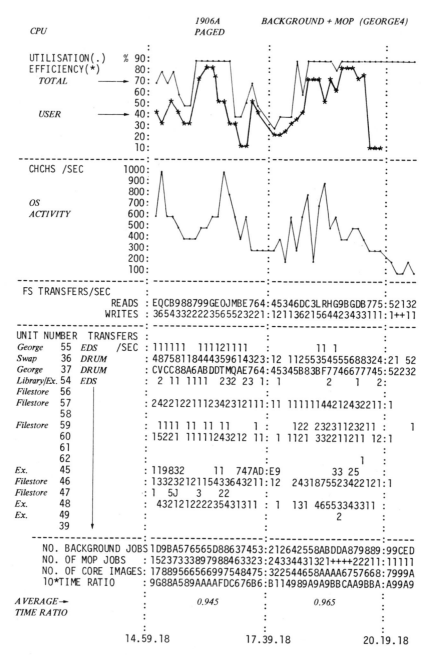

FIG. 1   An ongoing sizing method validation. TIME RATIO = time model
thinks it would take to do the work, divided by period length; one
space = eight minutes.

rounded to the nearest integer, and if you average these results over the 2 hour and 40 minute periods these provide values like .945, .965, and so on.

You've got there a way of playing with your modeling technique for your existing system, and so satisfying yourself about limits of accuracy. In this case, with the subset of all the data that we've used, we haven't got the data on magnetic tape utilizations here, and there is no data about any of the line printers and card readers, hence, for a short period, there could be bottlenecks. You get an indication here that for about half the time we were within five percent. Well, that's not too bad. What this indicates is that if we've got these measurements, then we can get quite close to the system throughout, and that is bound, I think, to change one's attitude towards the problem of the construction of benchmarks. Then one comes across to this question of how we do actually solve the problem we want to solve, because the basic problem behind benchmarking is to predict how the current workload will behave on some other system. Now this involves a two-way process. One has got, first of all, to take the existing workload and map it onto a machine-independent specification of that workload in terms of work units and total traffic expressed in kilobytes. Then one's got to do the reverse process of mapping it back onto some other hardware system that may have different blocklengths for the different traffic, and that you may assess and have a different number of kilobytes of core to support a process, and so on. In principle, these problems are not too difficult, and you can get very close to their solution. When we go about the job in that way, it leads us to reformulate the benchmark problem as the problem of model calibration. What we are really interested in is quite small benchmarks that will enable us to establish the calibration points of models. For example, there are two things that a drum transfer does. It loads the drum, but it also loads the CPU because of the operating system overheads involved in organizing the transfer, so you need a measure of the number of CPU instructions it takes to execute a drum transfer. Well, you can devise a little benchmark to measure that, similarly with these other things, and of course with the compiler efficiency. Now if you do all this you come very close to fulfilling what I take to be the objective of this college, whose motto is, "Happy is the man who understands the causes of things." That's really where we ought to be getting to.

There is just one more topic I'd like to raise, and that is the question of what users' workloads consist of. This theme has cropped up several times here, and it should be looked at from a manufacturer's point of view. One thing which is very striking is that a lot of the benchmarks we get don't represent the user's workload. So, leaving aside the political cases where it's all arisen as a result of some ghastly creed, I'm sure that you wouldn't seriously quarrel with me if I said that the CPU spends about the amount of time indicated in Fig. 2 on the user's program, and all of that inside various bits of the operating system. It also spends its time, quite a long time, in housekeeping; just deblocking logical records takes at least 40 instructions for every 100 characters, that sort of thing, compiling, of course, sorting, and other utilities. Now the chunk labeled *physical file management* is worth examining. Every time you access a record, at the very least 1000 instructions or thereabouts on large operating systems are examined. On a small system, such as some of the small DOS equivalent operating systems, this number falls to around 500 instructions.

From the manufacturer's side there is a big problem here, not just a technical problem, but a marketing problem, too. We just don't have enough feedback of the sort that we need, and we don't really know how to get that feedback, either. The sort of feedback we need to know is the relative importance of generality and rigidity. With

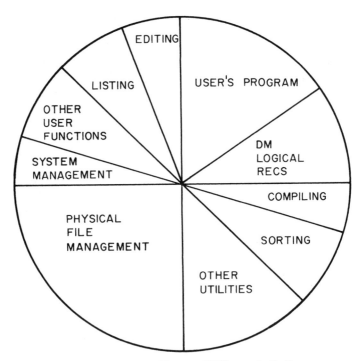

FIG. 2   Estimate of how a CPU spends its time.

the small operating systems, for example, you provide a relatively inflexible approach to physical file management, and you can manage to do it in 500 instructions. With the larger system, the flexibility and generality provided, together with such features as resilience, will cost more like 1000 instructions for the same physical file management function.

In Fig. 2, one can see that the computer spends some of its time editing. Some people say editing is part of the operating system, while others say it's on the user's side of the fence. With increasing data management facilities, we're going to get more sophisticated forms of editing, information retrieval, and so on, and altogether there are going to be more and more user functions.

To sum up, as manufacturers we would certainly agree that the day of the large, very expensive, very complex benchmark is over. It is just as expensive for us to run, and we don't mind admitting that point of view. We also believe it is very expensive from your point of view. On the other hand, it's clear that we need a small number of carefully designed and scientifically constructed benchmarks to evaluate these rates of exchange that I have mentioned. They will thus help us to support an altogether better sizing methodology based largely on appropriate modeling techniques. In that way we can become altogether more professional and more scientific about the whole sizing business, and hence we shall be able to get our benchmarking onto a more modest but a more competent footing.

DISCUSSION

F. J. M. Laver (Session chairman): I think we could perhaps take just a few points of information very quickly. We'll leave the main bulk of this question period until after the next speaker.

Unidentified speaker: Is the manufacturer prepared to make the measurement and modeling utility that Mr. Berners-Lee has described generally available?

Mr. Berners-Lee: Well, we're anxious not to make it generally available, of course, until it's been extensively used, but we've got to the stage now when we are pretty confident about this. We've been running courses teaching this methodology to our own systems analysis staff for some time, and we're just starting to begin to do the same for the customer, and it is all very fully documented.

Unidentified speaker: Have you planned your queuing models of thrashing behavior in order to give a more overall view?

Mr. Berners-Lee: Well, they fall very much into separate departments, for the following reasons: I think it's very clear, especially for the big system monitoring measurements, that thrashing is a very pathological condition. It only occurs very rarely, and then always in association with a particular program, such as one that accesses an array the wrong way around. I don't know if anybody else would like to comment on that in connection with thrashing, but my probable feeling is that too much is being made of the thrashing business. It's an occasional pathological situation which you can sometimes identify on the printouts. It's a transitory phenomenon associated usually with problems and programs that do crazy things.

Unidentified speaker: How does the total core required fit into your model?

Mr. Berners-Lee: The total core required fits into the model because one establishes the average core requirement of the process, and the total core available determines the level of concurrency that it would support.

Previous speaker: And you regard this as fixed for the life of a process?

Mr. Berners-Lee: For the life of a number of processes acting concurrently.

Previous speaker: Do you reckon that this is something that is probabilistic, or is it something that is strictly determined for a given period?

Mr. Berners-Lee: Oh, strictly determined for a given period.

Two Major Manufacturers' Attitudes towards Benchmarking–II

Robert Prendergast

Univac

I work mostly in the area of the larger 1100 machines, and there will obviously be a bias in what I say towards the large machine area, but most of it is applicable to the smaller scale machines. I'm not a benchmark specialist, but I shall attempt to say how the current benchmark situation has developed, what happens during a benchmark, the value of a benchmark, and, finally, what changes we would like to see. I would like to make it clear at this point we haven't a special benchmarking team, nor have we anybody whose sole objective in life is to tune up benchmarks. But why do we do benchmarks? We do them because our business is selling computer systems. When we do a benchmark, we expect that we can satisfy the criteria set by the customer better than anybody else, which eventually will sell a computer. I think everybody will agree with that; it's the simple answer to a simple question.

Somehow, from our point of view, benchmarking seems to have got right out of hand. Now I'll explain that. The original value of computers was the speed with which they could perform scientific calculations. When they were developed commercially and companies began competing with each other for business, it became necessary for the buyers of these machines to ask the normal questions: "How much is this?" "Does it do the job?" and then, eventually, "How fast is it?" The result of this is that various mixes such as Gibson and the

Post Office Work Unit Mix were developed. More sophisticated mixes came later that were more task oriented, and then software oriented, as this became more important. Fairly early on people began to say, "Well, how does this relate to me?" And the answer usually was, "I'm a special case; it doesn't relate to me." So, for those people who already had a machine, the problem was usually one of throughput: "How can I get a quart out of a pint pot, or how can I get an Atlas out of an abacus?" We found that many users were taking a number of jobs that typified their workload or, in some cases (and we've seen the Oxford Benchmark mentioned again), they were taking a whole shift of work and asking the manufacturer to run it on the machine that they proposed, the winner being the man that could run the fastest. It was at this point the arguments began, such as, "XYZ used a quick and dirty compiler," and, "ABC used a drum, but you wouldn't let us use a drum," and, "Ours is only slow because it's measured from first card in to last line out." This was the particular point about the Oxford Benchmark: if you wanted to put a fast card reader on or you wanted to put a fast printer on, you could alter your time quite dramatically. This is how the arguments went on.

Following this, quite a few people had their fingers burnt going from second to third generation or going from one machine to another, and the idea that you were taking your life in your hands if you changed machines gained some currency. On this basis, then, it was quite reasonable for people to ensure that if they did change that

    1. all the programs could be converted,

    2. the new machine could run them if you could convert them,

    3. it could do the additional tasks that had been claimed for it, and

    4. the new machine was faster.

The problem then was, and still is, what are you trying to prove? How good a conversion can you do, or how fast a conversion can you do? How important is the speed of the converted programs versus the new programs you are writing for it (because converted programs can be notoriously slow)? So you often ended up weighing one part of the benchmark against another, the quality-versus-quantity arguments.

Then, time-sharing, or multi-access as some people call it, hit us. This is similarly difficult to quantify in exact terms, and large demonstrations of time-sharing are almost logistically and physically impossible. So not many were performed. I'm still waiting to see benchmarks for all those 100- and 200-terminal networks that some users saw as an absolute necessity a few years ago.

I tested three major benchmarking areas, the large batch time-sharing area, the conversion area, and the standard packages area. We've talked about the first case a few times, how it's going out of fashion from one point, but from where we stand it's certainly not going out of fashion. These things keep cropping up. In the second case, conversion, most users are paying more and more attention to this. If they've made a considerable investment in programs, they obviously want to be able to take most of them over onto a new system. They also want to see if the manufacturer has the capabilities, expertise, and experience to help him convert to a new area. That's our new system. I think the third area, standard packages, is the most interesting, and it offers a great deal of scope for the benchmark enthusiast. In this area I include software packages for data-base management transaction processing systems and some of the larger application systems.

Normally when somebody is introducing a new system, especially when it involves a data base and/or transaction processing, they put several man years and a considerable investment into performing a feasibility study, producing a systems design, monitoring the programs. In fact, they do all the things that one normally does when faced with the production of a new system. It is well known that manufacturers are geniuses, that they can perform miracles and do the impossible, so they give us three months to do this in the form of a benchmark! What sort of a data base management system do you expect to see in that time? So what happens? From a very small beginning, this escalated into today's mammoth 20th-Century Fox type extravaganza, with ICL versus Univac in the battle of the data-base management systems.

I think most of them end up with some degree of dissatisfaction on both sides, whatever benchmark they have, because they tend to be amateurish efforts, and I don't really think they achieve their objectives. Now why does this happen? It happens when we're talking to a customer or prospective customer and eventually he says, "We want to do a benchmark." So we stand back aghast, but we agree to progress a bit further, and we get the benchmark documentation and a time scale with it. We look at what he wants us to do and the time scale, and usually when he's given it to us he says, "I'm sorry, I know it's a short time scale, but Value Added Tax is coming in in February," or something like that, and this determines the time scale. So we look at it, and usually we say, "You can't do it," but perhaps we come to a compromise or we agree to do it anyway. Then the benchmark material is delivered late. So when we get it, we start working on it—let's say it involves some tapes with some programs on—we start converting the tapes, and we find that after a few days one of the programmers comes back and says something like, "Look, I'm having a lot of trouble reading this tape," or, "The results we're getting from this program don't match up." So we spend another week looking at it, and eventually we just have to give up. We go back to the prospect and say, "Sorry, we just can't get any further, we can't make this program work." They say, "Oh yes, funny you should say that, so-and-so said that as well; you must have the wrong tape." So that's a week gone by. Then in time we perform 90 percent of the work within the time scale. The last 10 percent just can't be done in the time scale, so we say we must have an extension or we just drop that last 10 percent. This is likely to have happened with the other manufacturers, only the 10 percent they can't do is a different 10 percent. During all this time the user's or the customer's original team of four people has been whittled down to a stalwart one or two, but they can't keep pace with the demands put on them by the manufacturers. So we often have to wait days or even weeks to put a question and a similar period to get an answer. Now by the agreed benchmark's date we're not always ready. The programmer is a notorious optimist, and you can't stop him working up until the last minute. And it's quite often again we've done a modification on the spot, or a further extension. When it comes to running the benchmark, they can often go wrong, especially if you put together a new configuration because with a new configuration you would get a stability problem, the same as when you install a new machine. You don't expect the thing to run perfectly right from the word *go*. An even worse situation, though, is where you've just started running the benchmark, fingers crossed, your adrenalin's running, when the customer says, "Well, what about the XYZ factor?" Well, the XYZ factor is something that's never written down, that was so obvious that one party never thought it worth mentioning, it was just understood. And at that point you pray for the false floor to collapse. It could be something simple like the ability of the system to differentiate between user time and system overheads for tasks. It is possible on some systems, but not our systems. Then we run the benchmark. The user then ends up with a mass of information, which takes a hell of a long time to interpret. If you multiply this by the number of manufacturers in the exercise, you've got a problem, and I'm sure a lot of the output, in fact I know a lot of the output, is just ignored. It possibly just goes along to make up the number. The next thing that happens is the decision is delayed at least two months, even years, sometimes never. Finally we end up with a bunch of people completely exhausted who need a rest.

In most benchmarks 10 of those 11 situations will occur. You don't have to go very far to discover the causes. They're too ambitious. Normally we consider ourselves to be mortal, fallible human beings, but the tests we're asked to do often are flattering, but impossible. I'm sure this situation arises where a group of programmers arrive at the pearly gates having done a benchmark. You say, "Congratulations, you guys. It took us six days, you did it in five, but ICL got the business!" No commercial organization can expect people to accept as a regular mode of operation the long and difficult hours that benchmarks demand of people. Benchmarks are usually badly planned. Under normal circumstances your systems manager has said to you, "Here's a job; it'll take about 20 man years. Can you and Charlie complete it by the end of next month? You can have all the computer time between 2 and 4 in the morning, all Saturday evening, and all day Sunday." You might be a bit concerned about his state of mind and about his job security, perhaps your own. But we are faced with this situation time and time again when we do a benchmark. So what do you get out of a benchmark? The previous authors have said, "Very little," and I agree with them. What you hope to get and what you usually set off to do is to say which machine fits your future needs best within your budget. So you decide on a benchmark. But that's probably biased. I don't mean prejudiced; I mean it's probably based on your previous experience.

As I mentioned earlier, benchmarks and most other measures of performance are purely quantitative. They do not relate to the qualitative aspects of a system, such as its speed or its learning time or the quality of its compilers. What use is it to me, as a manufacturer, if I have a really superb compiler that, because of its diagnostic power, can get a job into production in 60 percent of the time of a normal compiler, if all you, the customer, are interested in is batch and time-sharing ratios? We are usually faced with multiple choices of software and hardware. If we get it right in time to run a benchmark we are lucky. We don't get much time for tuning. Thus we're never really sure whether we're getting the best cut of our benchmark because we often find that when we rerun, with a bit of maneuvering we can halve the time. You can see this on the Oxford Benchmark; anybody who's done it has halved his time when compared with his original time. I think, possibly, we got even lower than that. Some people resolve that by defining the software we will have to use, but really the same conditions apply. The last person you should have to define the test is the manufacturer of the goods that are going to be tested. I hardly expect we'll get to the situation where a member of the consumer magazine *Which?* anonymously attempts to purchase an 1106. I don't mind, but it's an anomaly that we are the supplier in a competitive situation, and we are also asked to be the independent tester.

I do not see how the computer community can afford to support the luxury of benchmarks for much longer, because the sums of money involved are enormous. Most are several thousand pounds, and it's not unknown, in fact it regularly happens, that they cost tens of thousands of pounds, but that includes the cost of labor and some computer time. The cost therefore is staggering. Customers often don't believe this until we go through the figures.

There's also an impact in terms of resources because major benchmarks demand the best people. So the best way to do a benchmark is not to have a benchmark, because they tend to draw people from normal support work. Thus if you're not careful you deplete the service that you give to your existing customers. Who suffers? We do directly, but then there's only one person who pays in the end. What are the answers? We haven't any solutions, but we'd like to see things change a little bit. I think there could be a considerable tightening up of the benchmark area to prevent all this waste, duplication, and reinventing of the wheel. Sometimes we feel a benchmark is purely for external appearances; my ICL colleague also thinks that, in some cases. The decisions are being made on criteria other than those specified, so when we do the benchmark most people have already made up their minds. Other times we are performing feasibility studies and providing expertise and systems designs. If you asked a firm of consultants to do this, which you should be doing if you are in the early stages of choosing a new system, then they'll charge you a fee. Similarly, if we are asked to do our benchmark, we should be paid on a time-and-materials basis for the work you want done. This way you will have proper management control, which will ensure a professional approach to the work on both sides. That's one constraint. But the benchmark should still not be called upon unless absolutely necessary. The buying and selling of a computer is a lengthy exercise. There are many points to consider, and the benchmark, at best, can only be a small part of this. If you find that it's at all necessary to run a benchmark, then only the preferred supplier should be asked. He is the man who has satisfied all the criteria, has received your technical recommendations; it is he who has been agreed upon by your board as being the best supplier. There may be something, though, that you're not quite sure about.

At that point the manufacturer can be asked to demonstrate any points that are causing concern for the buyer. A satisfactory demonstration will then ensure a sale.

DISCUSSION

Mr. Laver (Session Chairman): I would like a short discussion on the last two papers, and then we'll extend it afterwards.

Mr. Hatt: I notice you don't talk about the problem of the manufacturer in benchmarking his own machines during manufacture. This must be something to do with the nature of the inside of Univac, but I would have thought that Univac actually had people who thought about this from the point of view of testing the performance of the machines they're designing. Is this so?

Mr. Prendergast: Well, yes. I'm not from the manufacturing side, so I'm not exactly *au fait* with what they do. Yes, we do benchmark our machines, we do design benchmarks to test that they are meeting their performance criteria. Yes, we do design them to a certain specification to perform in a certain way, and we test to see that they are meeting their performance criteria.

Unidentified speaker: I think perhaps your view of benchmarking is a realistic one in the situation that faces you, but I do feel the problems lie as much with the specification of the benchmark as anything. I personally have been concerned with the specification of a benchmark for multi-access systems, and we didn't really have any of the problems that you mention. Of course, I wasn't on the manufacturer's side, so I didn't see some of the problems that may have arisen, but all the benchmarks ran successfully in a relatively short length of time. They all got the results out that we expected (that is, they all got numbers out; they weren't all, of course, what we expected, otherwise there wouldn't have been any point in doing it). Moreover, it was only done with a limited number of manufacturers, all of whom, if they had made it there, would have had the opportunity to take part.

Mr. Prendergast: Yes, part of the point I was making was this. In the competitive situation, in a very short time, you often only get one chance to benchmark, and that chance is too late. We've found quite a few times that, just by changing the hardware around a little, quite considerable gains in performance have been obtained. You never know in the benchmark situation whether you're doing as well as possible.

John Smallbone (Institute of Oceanographic Sciences [IOS]): One of the points that I think has been overlooked is the fact that a lot of customers are perhaps not as well informed about their workload as the manufacturers are about their own performances on different machines. You've already stated that by switching hardware around while working on the same benchmark, you can achieve quite considerable increases in performance. Wouldn't it be wiser for the user to give benchmarking information to the manufacturer in plenty of time so that if it's noticed that the proposed core isn't big enough then he can quickly slap on some more before he tenders? I also think that the customer should only approach one manufacturer in order to get the benchmark work carried out. There is the point, however, that if the customer only knows what jobs he wants done, perhaps the benchmark is itself meaningless, if he just takes it along and says, "This is my requirement."

I'll explain the situation I mean. The Institute of Oceanography is at present evaluating a medium scale machine. We are operating on four different machines over a variety of locations, and the benchmark that we have put together is intended to be representative of an envisaged workload that we have. I think we've already taken into account a lot of the points that have been put forward today about the difficulty of providing a representative workload in this work for the IOS. What we attempted to do was to put forward as representative as possible a workload that we could see, taking into account how the users might change and given ideal conditions for running their workload. I think there is a difficulty in establishing a representative workload that I fully recognize, having had to put this one together. I find it even harder to believe that any synthetic benchmark is going to be more representative than my representative benchmark. At least I understand fairly well where my representative benchmark might not be entirely representative; I would probably have a lot more doubts about a synthetic benchmark that I didn't completely understand.

Mr. Prendergast: I'm not convinced there's a need for any benchmarks in the competitive situation. In your situation I think what we could possibly do would be to do what Mr. Berners-Lee suggested earlier. If you tell us what your expected workload is, we can predict fairly accurately the sort of machine you'll require and the performance you'll get on that machine.

Mr. Smallbone: I think I can describe our position without going into too many details. When I entered the benchmark exercise, I was not completely convinced of its merit. We had to have some benchmark results for our evaluation, and so we were forced to undertake the exercise. We've already run two satisfactorily, and the other two are well in hand. The results that we have had so far have led us to believe that we have gained an awful lot from these benchmarks. At least one manufacturer that you would have thought would have had no difficulty has experienced difficulty. This is the sort of information that we could only really find out by running a benchmark, unless we were in a situation where we had that machine, and we started to do our workload, or we felt we'd made a classic boob.

Mr. Prendergast: Have you thought how much your benchmarks are costing?

Mr. Smallbone: Yes, that's a thing I'm very worried about, and I very much agree with your point.

Mr. Laver: The real question would seem to be what its cost is as a fraction of the total system cost. It's not its absolute cost, whether it's £1,000 or £10,000, that's important; it is relative cost when compared to the total system cost.

Mr. Smallbone: Yes, but you must remember that I'm a user, rather than a manufacturer, and if I am completely satisfied that the machine we have chosen is going to perform its task, then the benchmark is successful. Now, I'm also a conscientious user, so I appreciate the cost that's involved, and I would be very pleased if, as a result of this conference, we came up with some good ideas that would give customers satisfaction and confidence, if they learned precisely what they were doing with, say, a synthetic benchmark, especially if one would get around these problems.

I think, though, that one has to recognize that these problems exist when you are in the process of buying a new computer because it is such a big expenditure. There is always a very great deal of uncertainty about what the manufacturer's offering. This meeting is probably far more interested in benchmarking as a study, a general study or an aid to manufacturing, rather than its implications to a potential customer who is using the benchmark really to satisfy himself that he is buying the right machine.

Mr. Prendergast: There doesn't appear to be very much trust in these situations, I think. I detect that people don't trust the manufacturers. I don't think you trust each other, either. We often come across a situation where we have somebody who wants to buy a machine, and they say, "We want to do a benchmark," and so on.

We say, "Your work profile is very similar to that other user, and we've just done an exercise for him. Will you accept that as being a measure of our system performance?" And they say, "No, that's nothing like us." I don't believe that there are so many people around that are unalike. There is a similarity in systems. A lot of users do run very similar systems. There are slight differences, but their objectives are the same, their programs are often the same, but there are not many people who'll accept it, and they don't trust their fellow users.

Mr. Smallbone: Can I just say that of the four manufacturers that are active with the IOS benchmark, two have definitely proposed a different configuration from the one they were originally proposing, and a third one has gone down because they thought in the first place they were offering a CPU that was too fast for us, and they're offering us a lesser CPU. These represent to us greater savings than the cost of the benchmark.

Mr. Laver: I don't think I'm going to attempt to summarize what's been said. It's fairly clear that most people have doubts about the validity of benchmarking on what I'd call the grand scale, but we've got really to distinguish between two very different situations: the situation where people simply want to tune or tweak a little bit of their system and do some measurements or possibly move to a larger machine in the same family, and the entirely different situation where somebody is buying a new machine. I think there are much better ways of doing it, and I think that benchmarking is an expensive luxury in that second area that neither the manufacturer nor the customer, in most cases, can afford. Benchmarking at best is a very small component of the total process of picking a new machine. I have some personal views about benchmarks and the way they should be constructed, which I won't go into now.

Unidentified speaker: Mr. Prendergast seemed to be making the comment, what a hard life it is in this commercial world! Accepting that we should trust manufacturers and be prepared to take the word of their previous customers, and so on, are manufacturers prepared to back up their statements of how well their product will meet the objectives by some kind of guarantee and penalty clauses and this sort of thing?

Mr. Laver: Policy, rather than science.

Mr. Prendergast: No, I'm not a policy maker, so the answer is no.

Mr. Jones (Harwell): I would like to make a point about this business of getting hold of other users' information. We are members of one of the IBM users' associations. We get a great deal of information from other installations about what you can and you can't do on the various sizes of machine. IBM gets a great deal out of these associations, too. I'm not really sure what the situation is with other manufacturers, but I was wondering whether this is a possibility: is it possible for people who are not owners or renters of ICL equipment to get into these user groups, to be able to get the experience and share the experience of other people?

Mr. Berners-Lee: Yes, sure, come along, but the basic question that arises, I think, is: what's the BCS doing about this? Surely it's a function that the Society ought to be fulfilling?

Mr. Laver: I think there is also another problem: It's no good being too clever at measuring all these properties because the moment you install a new system, for example, your users will immediately learn the quirks of that new system with remarkable rapidity. It's about the only time programmers ever seem to wake up, actually, when a new system appears, and they've got to try and find out how to break it or how to deceive some of the nicer parts of the system. This can have a very dramatic and drastic effect on your total workload, and you've got to estimate with that sort of problem in mind. It's like putting a new computer into a management system; you know the thing, you think you've run your management that way for 20 years. You put in a computer and straight away your management system has to change almost inevitably, so you've got to bear this in mind. It's no good being clever and looking for very precise measures such as the nearest five percent, the nearest ten percent, because a lot of these other factors are going to be much greater than that in their effects and implications.

Unidentified speaker (ICL): Someone made a statement suggesting that manufacturers should underwrite their statements about the capability of the machine to do a workload. Would he be willing to underwrite his workload with them and the capability of our machine? It should be a joint exercise. We're both standing to lose.

Dr. Buttle (Exeter University): You're quite right, workloads do change, of course, and, as was pointed out from the chair, users will very rapidly adapt to a new situation. It still leaves you with the point: you want to know what a machine will do. The manufacturers will obviously try and tell you, or try and sell their thing, and if it's going to be on a matter of trust there are an awful lot of people who have gone bust or had a great deal of trouble with their systems. We would obviously be prepared to underwrite the specifications that we originally demanded.

ICL speaker: And the joint exercise?

Dr. Buttle: Speaking personally for Exeter, we're very pleased with the liaison with the company. Also, to take up a point from down there about the benefits from the users' group, we do, in fact get a great deal of feedback, and it is useful. I'm not being too cynical here, but it is a point that an awful lot of manufacturers sell an awful lot of equipment, and with antitrust suits and all sort of things, one is left wondering where poor little users stand when they're buying their first system.

Mr. Prendergast: I want to come back to your question of guarantees. I think the matter of degree of guarantee is hair-splitting a bit, but I think most manufacturers do produce a proposal where they evaluate the workload you've given them, and they'll produce a machine based on that. I think in most people's cases there's a genuine attempt to offer you a machine to meet your workload, although I believe again there is this suspicion that this is not always so.

To take up a point from over there that was about taking three years to evaluate a system: some people do take an awfully long time to evaluate systems, they take years, and they end up with a very good system but it's obsolete, and there are several cases of this around. That's not a bad thing; they have a perfectly adequate system, but it's running on what's now considered old hardware.

Mr. Laver: Let's not go into the discussion of what *obsolete* means and whether we ought to have to put up with the word *obsolete* floating around.

I'd like to try and steer the discussion back a little bit because there's an element of manufacturer-beating at the moment. I am not a manufacturer so I can safely say let's try and steer it back onto what the basis of the discussion should be.

Dr. J. G. Sime (Glasgow University): In answer to the gentleman from the University of Exeter, in the case of our contract for the 1906S, ICL has accepted a penalty clause if they fail to meet our benchmark requirements.

Mr. Sharp (British Gas): My question is mainly to Mr. Prendergast. Given the manufacturer's unwillingness to carry out benchmark testing, how does he suggest that a customer should assess where the system proposed by a manufacturer will, in fact, meet requirements which he, the customer, knows? Would it meet Mr. Prendergast's objection if customers agreed to pay fixed amounts to each manufacturer invited to make a proposal for a system, to cover the cost of preparing that proposal and carrying out any necessary benchmarking?

Secondly, can I say on a somewhat different point, it seems to me it would be very helpful to customers if manufacturers would make available to them the software that I assume they must, themselves, possess, that they use to configure systems, so that the customer can evaluate for himself perhaps an enhancement to the system that he has by evaluating various alternatives? If that isn't done he is in danger of reinventing the wheel, trying to devise a way in which he can decide whether to add more core or more discs, or decide whether he needs a faster drum. The manufacturer has these tools for making these decisions available. Why are they not made more freely available to customers?

Mr. Prendergast: I don't know if I gave the wrong impression. I'm not entirely against benchmarking; I'm very much against bad benchmarking, and most benchmarking is bad benchmarking. I think the cost element will help to make people have some real objectives before using it, it will make them wonder if they really want to do it. It will make them think about what they're trying to do, and it will make the thing much more professionally run, which they're not at the moment. I don't have any answers to the benchmarking situation. I think the question of evaluation is very difficult if you want to take it to the detailed level, the sort of level that we've been talking about at times here. I don't think it's necessary always to take it to the detailed level.

The next question was about the software we have for evaluating our hardware and software. As far as I know, anything that is a proper product of ours is available to the customer. Obviously, if it's a program that somebody's just knocked up to test a disc or a tape unit or a particular part of the operating system, no, it's not available because we have terrible problems supporting things like that.

Mr. Berners-Lee: I'd like to follow on the last question. I think really the answer to your question is that it's rather too early for this. I don't think we ourselves have been using these tools for long enough, and that in due course this will happen, I'm sure the users will use these, and I think it will probably start from the consultants. I hear no mention of the use of consultants, but after all, in the building business if you want a house built you go to an architect and he puts the plans to the builders. One would have thought that we should eventually get to the stage where that happens more often than it does now in the computer business and especially in the case where a specialized technique of assessment is required.

Mr. Prendergast: Just going back to that question of measurements in our software, to reinforce what Mr. Berners-Lee said, yes it is very early days for this, and we're not entirely satisfied with it ourselves. There are hardware and software monitors. When we've looked at some of these, it takes an incredible amount of study to work out what is really happening. I think perhaps we feel that the users may not always interpret it in the way it should be interpreted.

Roger Jeffereys (Burroughs Machines Ltd.): I usually deal with 6700s. I think I want to enforce what the last speaker said. I should say, too, that I'm on the benchmarking team of Burroughs. One of the things that I think troubles us most is when a user comes to our team and presents us with a benchmark that tests his current configuration. It takes no account of the fact that Burroughs' structure inside the machine is completely different, the whole concept of the way things are done in the Burroughs machine is different. So we start complaining about some of the effects that we see in the benchmark that is presented to us, and these effects have never occurred to the user. In other words, what I'm saying is, some people's complexity is other people's simplicity. We have a very complex machine. It has a complicated paging mechanism, it very frequently is a multi-processor machine, it does multi-tasking either at the user level or at the MCP level. When you start throwing all these extra parameters in, the user either doesn't want to know or doesn't like to take the effort to understand the effects that this will have on his benchmarks. We feel sometimes that we are a little bit out in the cold with our complex structures. They are not difficult to use, but the effects that they show are not easily understood.

Mr. Berners-Lee: I can give a current situation where the benchmark that we are being constrained to use makes a sophisticated operating system operate in an extraordinarily crude way because the competition does it that way in that particular case.

Unidentified speaker: I'm told that Rolls Royce says that the power of some of their machines is sufficient. Can we look forward to the day when computer manufacturers can simply tell us the same?

Mr. Laver: I think you have to ask the inevitable question, sufficient for what? You hardly want them sticking RB2 11s in cars. Might be fun to drive, though.

The Design of Multi-Access Benchmarks–I

R. G. Bayly

ICL

I'd like to make a sort of statement about benchmarks. I think everybody here has heard the story about the princess and the pea. It only needed the pea to find the princess, and I hope in your search your benchmarks will be more like peas than like boulders or stones!

I intend to concentrate on benchmarks and their use in systems evaluation—not competitive evaluation, but evaluation of the existing or planned systems. This, you may think, limits what I say and may, therefore, not have much impact on what you are here for, but I believe that the rules and the rationale that I shall present actually apply. At the same time, it is aimed at one purpose, performance evaluation, and thus there is no competition, there is no helter skelter.

To start with, and to start in a literary vein, since we are at Cambridge (or maybe I should be at Oxford for this), I'd like to quote from the dictionary. "A benchmark is a point of reference for the purpose of levelling." As you might guess, that doesn't actually apply to computer benchmarks—or does it? If you use the term *levelling* as an expression to mean matching or balancing, you can see that the definition, which actually refers to surveying, is very appropriate, and that is the main purpose of any performance evaluation exercise. We're not trying to find out whether we can actually achieve the earth, or anything like that. We're trying to solve a sort of equation. On the one hand we have a workload, and on the other hand we have a system to handle that workload. What we're trying to do is set up the mechanism and design the tools that actually help us to solve that equation. Only by solving that equation can we actually ensure that we have the right system to do the job, and benchmarking is only one of the many tools that can be used and are used to solve that equation.

If we are going to use benchmarking or any other technique for performance evaluation, what sort of policy should we have? I would like to say what it means to make this sort of decision, this sort of use of a benchmark. If we're talking about a benchmark as a point of reference, it's no good as a point of reference of yesteryear. At the worst it must be a point of reference of yesterday, and at the best, of tomorrow or next month. So we've got to keep it up-to-date, and if you're going to do performance evaluation it's got to be a continuous process. Your workload's changing, the system's changing, the users are changing. You've got to change with them, and if you're going to use a benchmark it's got to change with all these other changes. So we have to continuously develop our benchmark.

One of the useful purposes of a benchmark—I use the term *benchmark* here quite loosely—is the ability to evaluate a suite of programs or an application system that, in fact, hasn't been currently implemented. You may need to decide what actions you will take to satisfy the requirements to actually put a particular application on your system. You can guess at it, you can suck it and see, but the best method is to actually do an evaluation. When I say you *benchmark it*, you actually define it in benchmark terms. You define the program, you define all the characteristics of the application, and you then use fairly ordinary techniques, a paper and pencil method together with analytical techniques and even simulation, to actually decide on whether or not this application will fit your system. It's an old scientific trick, actually, to use benchmarking as an evaluation of a design, and the reason it's used is for cost effectiveness. It isn't an extravaganza, it's actually applied to save money. Well, one of the things that you have to ensure, if you're going to use benchmarking for evaluation of future applications, is that your systems design and your systems designer are constrained to actually forecast what the systems are going to do. I think in the current day and age there seems to be a great deal of laxity on all sides toward defining what a particular program will actually do, how many instructions it will obey, how many transfers and how much core it will take, etc. We must return to some greater degree of rigidity in our definitions of systems to enable evaluation to take place at the earliest possible stage and to enable management decisions on how to use, control, or develop the system to be taken in adequate time.

I've said that we're talking about an evaluation of changes, not necessarily changes of machinery, but changes of workload, because you've got to take both into account. Some of the benefits from this are indirect because if you decide to use this technique, you have to do certain things, and it's the doing of these things that is beneficial. The benefits of benchmarking include:

1. A representative sample of the current workload is always available.

2. A continuous monitoring of the system takes place and thus changes in usage characteristics are identified early.

3. The need for control of usage by charging or restriction is identified quickly.

4. The limiting factors or components of a system become apparent earlier.

Well, I've meandered around the general field of benchmarking like everybody else, and I will now move rapidly on to multi-access. Before I start I ought to say that Dr. Sutcliffe and myself can't agree on what multi-access means, but here is our compromise definition:

Multi-access: a mode of use of a system enabling many users to independently interact with the system apparently with the total system resources and facilities at their disposal.

I think it has most of the aspects of the many definitions that go together.

What do we have to do to undertake a multi-access benchmark? It's much the same as any other benchmark. There are actual implementation differences and design differences, but the overall design follows the same sort of pattern. These are the steps that have to be taken and the decisions that have to be taken when undertaking a benchmark: First, and this is very important, setting the benchmark objectives. There's no point in undertaking a benchmark if you don't know what you're doing it for. On a fairly high level we say we want to know whether we've got enough room to put in a new application that some user department we're supporting requires. That's not the sort of objective I'm talking about. It's important to actually identify your real objective, the deep-down objectives—you know, wishy-washy things, like, "We need a new system." You've got to identify what you need it for, and I think the other authors have stressed this. It is impossible to actually do an evaluation if you really haven't got to the root of the problem. Evaluation in terms of multi-access is slightly different. We again want to know how much or how often we can do things, but we need to know certain other things. For instance, we may want to know what impact a multi-access workload would have on an existing batch load. This is one of the problems that bedevil most people who are moving to multi-access for the first time. We want to know what would happen if we allowed a particular group of users some greater latitude in their use of the multi-access facilities.

These are the sort of things that you may wish to use multi-access benchmarks for, and since you can't actually get all the users seated at their consoles practicing while you orchestrate them like the Hallé, you have to do it in a rather mechanical fashion. I agree with other authors who have said there is no replacement for the real human, but, unfortunately, we cannot afford the luxury of experiments with real humans. It's rather like heart surgery—you can't practice on your patients as you might kill them.

So what have we done? We've decided on the objectives, and now we've got to go on to the definition of the benchmark itself, rather an important point. In a multi-access set-up, when you are only evaluating the multi-access system, you need only define the multi-access part, but in most cases we are actually talking about a mixed system. I consider the use of programs to emulate the work done in the background to be an appropriate way of actually defining those background programs. The reason I say this is that the major problem with programs supplied by customers to manufacturers for benchmarks is that we can't understand them. They come in in rather funny languages, and they're in funny codes, and the worst thing is that the data is rather peculiar. We do have some rather strange differences between ourselves, and we can't actually understand the data, and I think it's mostly the data that's the problem. By removing the data element and emulating the programs—and by *emulating* I mean that the program exhibits to the outside world all the characteristics of the real program—you can get a good representation of the workload. It actually does it with funny data, and it's written in a fairly standard high-level language with the ability to exhibit detailed characteristics of the original program. It isn't the workload, I won't say it is in any way, but it's enough to give you a good feel for what the impact will be. It gives you directionality.

What are the elements in the definition of the multi-access part of the benchmark? Well, there are two main components. The number of terminals involved (which could be from one to one hundred or two hundred and maybe, if the estimates for the future are correct, thousands) is one variable that has to be defined. We can do two sorts of evaluation; we can say how many terminals this system can support, say, "We don't know how many terminals we want; how many can you give us?" The second, and probably the better, approach is to ask, "What will happen if I put 12 terminals on the system?" And so on and so forth. So that's one of the variables. When I'm talking about terminals, I'm talking about them in the benchmark sense—connected terminals. You may install these 1,000 terminals spread all over the United Kingdom. The actual use of the terminals may be limited to remain well below the number of terminals that actually exist. Whenever I refer to the *number of terminals* throughout the rest of the section, or if Dr. Sutcliffe does in his section, we mean concurrent terminals, concurrently active terminals.

The second variable is that difficult one, the workload, and it has to be defined in some way or other. What we're trying to do in a multi-access benchmark is to define what the users are actually doing on the terminals. It's a very difficult task, but here are some of the aspects. There's the typing time. How long does the user take to type this load of rubbish in? There's the thinking time. Does he sit there drinking his coffee between each message? There's the session length. Does he sit on his terminal all day long? There's a number of active terminals. How many users are there out in the world? We need an expression of the number of active terminals; we need the mean and the peak. We may be willing to accept a system that will support 20 terminals with the required responsiveness, and take the rough 25 terminals as they come. We may always want to provide a service of a particular level, and then we'd have to do peak evaluation. These considerations involve the user himself. Then we have to find out how he uses a system. What types of interactions does he use? Does he want to compile programs, edit files, do interrogations of large data bases? What does he do? How many times does he do it? I've called it *data volumes*, but it's really a complexity factor. You can say he does compilations, but are they 10-line programs or 1,000-line programs? We have to identify some complexity factor. These are the sort of characteristics that we have to determine of both the user and how he uses the system.

We present the work done in a thing called a *script*. Figure 1 is an example of a script. It's a very poor script, as you've noticed;

```
 1   10   RP NONE
 2   20   IN BASICFUNK.T////
 3   10   NEW PROGRAM
 4   15   10 PRINT "THIS PROGRAM WILL USE STANDARD FUNCTIONS"
 5   15   20 PRINT "PLEASE INPUT ANY VALUE UNDER 10"
 6   15   30 INPUT N
 7   15   40 IF N < 10 THEN 71
 8   15   50 PRINT "PLEASE MAKE N LESS THAN 10"
 9   15   60 GOTO 30
10   15   71 PRINT "ABS(N)="
11   15   72 PRINT ABS(N)
12   15   73 PRINT "ATN(N)="
13   15   74 PRINT ATN(N)
14   15   75 PRINT "COS(N)="
15   15   76 PRINT COS (N)
16   15   77 PRINT "EXP(N)="
17   15   78 PRINT EXP(N)
18   15   79 PRINT "INT(N)="
19   15   81 PRINT INT(N)
20   15   83 PRINT "LOG(N)="
21   15   84 PRINT LOG(N)
22   15   87 PRINT "SGN(N)="
23   15   88 PRINT SGN(N)
24   15   89 PRINT "SIN(N)="
25   15   91 PRINT SIN(N)
26   15   92 PRINT "SQR(N)="
27   15   93 PRINT SQR(N)
28   15   96 STOP
29   15   ////
30   20   BASIC BASICFUNK(=0)
31   15   RUN
32   20   9.9
33   20   BYE
40   20   ED BASICFUNK(=0),JEANFUNK(1)
41   20   P1, (I/1./,T1)E
42   10   E
43   30   ED JEANFUNK(1),JEANFUNK(2)
44   15   (TC/PRINT/,R/PRINT/TYPE/)E
45   10   E
46   20   ED JEANFUNK(2).JEANFUNK(3)
47   14   T/1.30/,R/INPUT/DEMAND/
48   14   T1,P1,I/1.41 TO 1.71 IF N < 10
49   14   /,T1,R/GOTO/TO/
50   14   T3,(R/ATN(N)/ARG(N,10)/,T1)*2
51   14   T4,(R/INT/IP/,T1)*2
```

FIG. 1   Sample of a benchmarking script.

actually, the second page is not included in the figure, so it cuts off in the middle of the edit.

A script is a representation, in this case a statistical representation, of what the users are actually doing at the terminals. It tries to reflect two things. On the one hand it tries to reflect the types of interaction involved. On the other hand it tries to reflect some of the user characteristics. If you look at this script you will see that each line is preceded by two numbers; the first number, as you can see, is just an ordinary sequence number; the second is what we call the *think time*. The think time is a representation of the time that the user spends sitting at his terminal doing things that have no impact on the system. This is the time he spends considering what he should do next, considering why the system told him that the last interaction is a load of rubbish, and things like that. It is also the time he spends actually typing. If you're thinking and typing, typing in computer terms is very slow. Think time really represents a time when the terminal is making no demand on the system. It's not tuned for anything, it's not waiting for anything. The rest of each line of the script is an actual interaction. You can see that a BASIC program was introduced, compiled, and run. When we got fed up with BASIC, we went on to JEAN, an ICL language.

How do we determine the script? How do we produce one? It seems to be the thing we're measuring. Well, it's just as difficult as defining any other workload, unfortunately. We do have some help in this, in that most systems actually produce job journals or systems journals which, under analysis, will yield the goal that must be achieved. What you try to establish, either manually or by using the machine, is what interactions are actually taking place, as well as the time between interactions when the user is not doing anything whatever. You try to obtain a full assessment of the whole system. Normally, the method used is to do it on a department-by-department basis and amalgamate the results at the end. However, the problems that arise when you have a number of different scripts of different types are acute. If, instead, you amalgamate them into one script to give a full representation, and you run them from every terminal, as long as the workload is actually representative and reflects the uses it will be okay. So if you've got an existing multi-access system you can actually sum the statistics of the jobs running in your system, and you can find out what your script should be.

What happens if you don't have one, and you're thinking of having a multi-access workload on what is essentially a batch machine? Well, you have to do some sort of a statistical analysis again. You do it principally on the batch work that is being undertaken by the system and try to map that onto a script. You say, this is what we do in batch mode, what would it be like in multi-access mode? It's a difficult operation, but it gives you a good estimate of what the multi-access script will be like.

We can't get to our goal in one stride, so we have to refine the work as time goes on. How do you get the think times in this case? We were able previously, when we had a system, to get the think times from the journals. How do you estimate what the think times will be? Well, you can do this by reference to a number of papers (everybody seems to be writing about think times), some of which may reflect your workload and your users. Or you can do it my way, which is to take a rule of thumb that says there is one second for each character that is typed. It sounds like a lot but it reflects most of the work that we've done quite accurately. It is also backed by that august body, Leeds University. They conducted some experiments which indicate that an allowance of about 1 second per character, rising to 1.9 seconds for more elaborate work, is about right.

For a completely new workload you've got a much more difficult problem. You've got to find the script from nowhere, as it were, and one thing I would suggest is for you to go to somebody else who has similar problems and who has actually got some multi-access systems. I'm sure that any manufacturer would direct you to such a person, and even the British Computer Society would be of some help. So what you're trying to do is to find the script from somewhere else. The other way of doing it, of course, is to get out the manufacturer's manual referring to how you use the multi-access terminal and map one out for yourself or map a few.

That defines the workload and how we get to it. The next step is defining the environment that we undertake the benchmark in or where we're actually modeling or simulating the benchmark. This involves certain other factors that put rigor on the benchmark: the file placement, the method of submission, the time table, the control system, the controls that you're going to set on this benchmark; so the total result is a full definition of the benchmark. As I said previously, the definition should, if at all possible, refer to just one script.

We'll go on to the criteria, now. You can't have any multi-access criteria without referring to the response time. We all define it differently, so you should get a definition of what you mean by response time and what we mean by response time and what your next door neighbor means by response time. My definition is:

Response time: the time that elapses between the depression of the send key and the output of the first character of message which terminates the interaction.

It's wise to establish the criteria before you actually undertake the benchmark because if you don't, the results influence your decisions.

Always say what it is you're aiming for before you get there, otherwise you change your mind. If we've got a situation where we can trade off, where, for example, there's a multi-access system with a background workload, if we don't state as criteria that the background workload should not be degraded by more than 20 percent, and the response time should not be greater than five seconds for a typical interaction type X, we get into troubles. We could easily make it 20 percent, 30 percent, or 40 percent; or we could make the response time one second, five seconds, or ten seconds.

How are the criteria stated? Well, unfortunately, response time is not one single number. It is a variable, so we have to use statistical measures to actually define it. Once you've decided what sort of measure you want, and that would be dependent on your particular requirements, you may be worried if a constant response time is important, or you may be worried in case you get too high a response time. You would choose your criteria on an appropriate basis. Once you've chosen the type of criterion then you can actually put some absolute measure against it, like, "I wish to have a mean responsiveness to type interaction X of so much." If you've done the execution right, the evaluation is no problem at all, and you can use whatever technique you wish to decide whether the criteria have been met. Look at the criteria, and if you have only just met them, try some variation. If, however, you've met them by a mile, then you can have some confidence in them. If you're just on the edge, try changing the number of terminals, try changing the think time slightly. We've found that changing the think time can have a significant impact on the capability of the system or the degradation caused to other parts of the system.

The Design of Multi-Access Benchmarks–II

Stuart E. Sutcliffe

ICL

A technique for determining the multi-access handling capability of a particular system must include evaluation against the following attributes:

1. *Controlled environment.* In order to examine the way in which a system reacts to configuration enhancements and changes in workload characteristics, a controlled environment must be produced. By this I mean that the evaluation must be repeatable and that a steady state condition must exist. In the case of measurements, one must run the system for a period before starting to record the results.

2. *Hardware requirements.* The hardware required for a particular technique may not be available for an evaluation exercise.

3. *Machine independence.* Whether a technique is machine-independent or not does not affect the user of the technique as much as it affects the justification for developing that technique.

4. *Response time recording.* Mechanisms for response time and resource utilization recording are, of course, necessary.

5. *Accuracy.* The accuracy of the results should be stated. This is dependent upon the validity of the workload definition, the assumptions made in setting up an exercise, including file distribution, etc., and the accuracy of the technique.

6. *Fixed-mode workloads.* When the system is not dedicated to multi-access work, the technique must be able to cope with batch and/or transaction processing work simultaneously.

7. *Development costs.* The cost, of course, must always be considered. This may involve the user in both the cost of developing tools and techniques and the evaluation exercise itself.

8. *Evaluation costs.* There are two types of techniques, those that involve measurement on the actual systems and those of prediction.

Measurement techniques can be divided into two types, those that involve humans to operate terminals and those that use a system exerciser, or a stimulator, as our friends across the water call it. Prediction techniques can be divided into three types: analytical, queuing theory, and stimulation models. I will briefly discuss the pros and cons of each technique.

First, measurement using human operators. They make mistakes, they deviate from the script, typing rates are inconsistent, they improve with experience, and, as the user parts of the interaction reduce this, the load on the system increases and you change the system that you are supposed to be measuring. A controlled environment is therefore difficult to achieve. A full configuration has to be available with all the terminals ideally located in one room. Response time recording and collating the results may prove a problem. If the operating system does not record these, perhaps a front-end processor, if there's one on the system, can be made to do so. Stopwatches are a last resort. Resource utilizations would normally be recorded by the normal software or hardware monitors of the system. The cost of mounting the evaluation exercise for, say, 50 terminals could be extremely high when 50 people are required for training and measurement sessions.

The use of a system exerciser obviates the necessity for any people and the use of the terminals themselves. An exerciser usually consists of a program that is resident in either the main frame or a front-end processor. In both cases it must communicate with the operating system in the main frame and appear to be n terminals. It must issue messages as if they came from independent terminals and implement the user think time. This has to include the time for the output of the last message, typing time, think time (which has not overlapped with any other part of the user interaction), and line delays. The exerciser can be used to log response times. A separate program can be used to analyze these when the measurement period has been completed. If you're using an exerciser, it is fairly straightforward to produce a controlled environment. A particular think time can be associated with each message, or random variables can be used, the think time being drawn from an exponential or other distribution with a specified mean value.

One possible problem that might be encountered when trying to achieve repeatable results is the state of the on—line file store at the commencement of the run. In systems where the operating system allocates the physical location of new files, the distribution of the benchmark files for across drives will be different from run to run. The practical effect of this is rarely significant, however. Exercisers are unlikely to be compatible with different manufacturers' hardware and are also dependent on suitable hooks being provided in the operating system.

The cost of monitoring an evaluation exercise can be high. Dedicated machine time is required for development of the benchmark, the measurement period, and configuration changes. Additional machine time is required to analyze the results.

There are some major differences between main-frame and front-end processor resident exercisers. Clearly a main-frame resident exerciser does not need additional hardware. However, if a site does not have a front-end processor then one has to be brought in especially for the evaluation exercise in order to use that technique. Response times can easily be stored in the main frame. The front-end processor may not have these storing or printing facilities. If it uses the main-frame to store these response times, it is no longer independent of the system it is measuring. Transportation and interface problems are likely to be greater with a front-end processor resident exerciser. Copies of the main-frame resident exerciser can be used on an unlimited number of sites simultaneously. A front-end processor resident exerciser may not need hooks in the operating system, and also it's likely to use the communication segments of the operating system. The main-frame exerciser falls down on both these counts. The main disadvantage of main-frame resident exercisers is that, as they are requiring resources of the system they are measuring, they may affect its performance. These overheads must be reduced to a very low level.

Before passing on, it's worth noting that exercises have additional uses. They can be used to tune operating system parameters, to determine the best location of residences of the operating system and file distribution, to determine the life expectancy of a given configuration, to determine the system bottleneck, and also to test new software. Often it is required to determine the capability of a system that one cannot get access to because it's still on the drawing board or the required configuration doesn't exist or it's unavailable. In these cases, or because the cost of undertaking a measurement exercise is too great, one must turn to prediction methods.

Analytical techniques can be purely theoretical or based on empirical results—for example, those obtained from using an exerciser. They can be of simple paper-and-pencil type or more complex computerized models. Individual response times are not provided by analytical techniques. Indications of mean response times, however, can be produced. The accuracy of the results is tied to the validation of the technique with measured systems. Interaction with batch or transaction processing workloads is not easy to achieve in an analytical model. The great advantage is that the use of an analytical method is relatively inexpensive, and a simple analytical technique should be used for all evaluation exercises to provide the initial configuration and to check results of other techniques. Classical queuing and Markovian models are often used to model transaction processing systems. Multi-access systems differ from dedicated transaction processing systems, and they have great randomness and spread of workload characteristics, whereas message resources in transaction processing systems are less varied and more predictable. Representing interactions between resources, CPU, disc, main store, etc., the operating system, its scheduling strategies, resource requirements, workloads consisting of all types of commands from compilations to interactive editing, mixed workloads of batch and transaction processing and multi-access, make a fully comprehensive mathematical model difficult to achieve. Validation of the technique with practical measurement is essential.

Simulation modeling can provide a flexible means of performance prediction. The development of a detailed model that incorporates the necessary interactions is expensive and time-consuming. It is unlikely that development can be justified for a single evaluation. Providing a suitable model does exist, the implementation for a particular project is likely to be less than the setting up of an exerciser, so it's likely to be quicker. A simulation model does not have problems due to lack of hardware availability. A CPU of infinite processing power can easily be benchmarked using a model. Validation is essential if one is to have confidence in the results.

To summarize then, measurement techniques are accurate in that they accurately record what happened, but the accuracy of the conclusions is dependent on that of the workload using the tests. Does it represent what's going to be actually run in a year's time, in two years' time, or when? The main disadvantage with measurement is that it takes a long time to collect the component jobs and set up the benchmark, make the measurements and evaluate the results. Prediction is a necessity when the system does not exist anywhere or any essential element is unavailable. No technique is best suited to all evaluation exercises, and a separate decision must be taken to determine the best technique for each exercise. The decision is constrained by the following: the availability of tools, the availability of a configuration, the time scale, and the allowable expenditure. My advice is: always use a quick analytical technique—it provides a starting point, and it's a check on other methods. Does a comprehensive and validated analytical technique exist? If the answer's yes and it's accurate enough for your purposes, then use it. Is the system available for the measurement project? Can we afford and justify the cost of measurement? If we answer yes to both these questions then one must check whether simulation techniques are available. Does a validated simulation model exist? Is the level of accuracy acceptable? Can we afford and justify the time and cost of using a model? If we answer yes to these three questions, and the measurement option is open, then one has to make the decision on cost effectiveness of the alternative methods. If one cannot measure the actual system, and a comprehensive model isn't available, can one afford and justify the time and cost of developing such a model? If the answer's no, then we're left with a simple analytical technique with all its shortcomings. This situation, of course, should never arise.

At ICL, all the techniques previously mentioned have been used, and I shall now describe three implementations, each using different approaches: an exerciser, an analytical technique, and a simulation model. First, the main-frame resident exerciser. The George 3 Operating System for ICL 1900 series processors enables a program resident in main store to communicate with it in such a way that a program can appear to be a large number of independent terminals. A typical exerciser sends messages to the operating system as if the user had typed them. It implements the user think time, and it records the response time from the operating system in a disc file. A separate program analyzes response times after the measurement period has been completed, and the mean standard deviation, 90-percent probability response time, etc., are provided for each message passed. Resource utilizations are produced by the standard George 3 software monitor. Main-frame overleads are minimized by adding main store to accommodate the exerciser. The communications processing parts of the operating system are replaced by the command issuer handling, which has approximately similar resource requirements. We have carried out well over 100 runs using such an exerciser with different CPUs, main store sizes, secondary storage configurations, numbers of terminals, user think times, settings of operating systems, tuning variables, multi-access workloads, and concurrent batch workloads.

Instead of carrying out an exhaustive and costly set of tests for every investigation, the results obtained by using the exerciser have been generalized in the form of a set of simple formulae and data tables. The different types of multi-access workload can be evaluated, and the method allows the use of batch workload concurrently. Anyone using this technique can substitute his own workload user think time and configuration. They can also have confidence in the results as the method is based on hard data taken from practical systems. Clearly, extrapolation can only go so far without loss of accuracy.

In addition, it is necessary to predict the performance of new machine architectures and operating systems. For such cases we use simulation models. At ICL we have three major simulation modeling systems, all of which have been described in the literature (Clark & Wisneiwska, 1971; Sutcliffe, 1972; and Cussons & Broadribb, 1973). My own model, known as MACSIM in ICL, was initially designed to study dedicated multi-access and combined multi-access and batch systems. I shall briefly describe it.

It's a discrete event simulation model which consists of a single Fortran program of 2500 statements. The program vets the input data, carries out the simulation, and outputs ongoing results on a final analysis. It requires less than 50 percent of the time it simulates if run on a CPU of the same power as is being simulated. Job-mix, operating system overheads, and hardware variables are all input parameters to the model, and various outputs, including individual response times, response time analyses, and resource utilizations, can be produced from this approach.

To get a feel for the way the model works, I'll give a talk-through of the handling of a message from a multi-access terminal. A message enters the main frame from a terminal and is held in a queue as a process awaiting main store. It may already have main store from the last interaction. Scheduler 1 may roll out a program to make space in main store. The process is then allocated a CPU time slice. Scheduler 2 selects a process with a time slice that is not suspended awaiting some event. The process then uses the CPU until a data transfer is generated and either the process is completed or it's pre-empted by the operating system to handle a data transfer interrupt. This, in turn, may result in a higher priority program gaining the CPU.

Alternative scheduling algorithms are built into the model. When a process generates a data transfer request, an entity is created called an activity. The activity is placed on a queue for the required device. In the case of a disc, when it reaches the head of the queue a seek is initiated, if required. When the seek is completed, the activity queues for the controller. When it gets to the head of the queue the end of transfer time is calculated, and when this occurs the data transfer is completed. If the process generating the activity was suspended awaiting the data transfer, then the process is de-suspended. In this way contention for the resources, randomness of user demand, interactions between processes, and effects of cumulative delays are represented. This model has been validated against results obtained from measuring actual multi-access systems.

Having mounted an evaluation exercise, it is essential to be able to interpret the results and to draw the correct conclusions. Results from one set of variables, fixed workload, fixed number of multi-access users, fixed mean think-time, and a fixed configuration don't yield much information. What we need to know is the effect of growth in demand, the ultimate system bottleneck, selection of planned enhancements and their effects in terms of improved cost performance and cost effectiveness. By plotting resource utilizations and response times, a graphical representation of the system performance can be built up. By plotting families of curves together, the sensitivity of the system to configuration and workload changes can be seen. I'd like to illustrate the principles that we've talked about by showing some results. These have been obtained from the evaluation exercises which we've actually carried out.

A typical configuration used for multi-access work is shown in Fig. 1. I've left off magnetic tape and basic peripherals. I guess people do use these things! They're not too important from our point of view. The workload consists of typical program development with file manipulation and Algol compilations. Fig. 2 shows the results that are obtained by varying the number of concurrent users.

The main store requirement of the largest program, the Algol compiler in this case, is 20 K words. Several runs have been carried out with different numbers of users each working through the same script, but starting at different points. Resource utilizations are shown in Fig. 3.

The workload on this configuration produces a CPU limited system. When the system is saturated, increased numbers of users

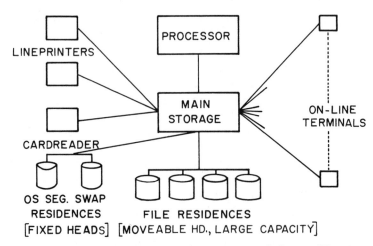

FIG. 1 Typical computer configuration used for multi-access
         work.

share the same amount of main store, and this leads to a main store
limited situation with a CPU utilization and throughput below its
optimum level.

In order to show the effect on response times, I have selected
the mean response time to message classes as the most relevant

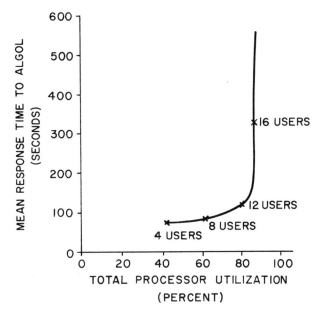

FIG. 2 Results of varying number of concurrent users
         in multi-access work.

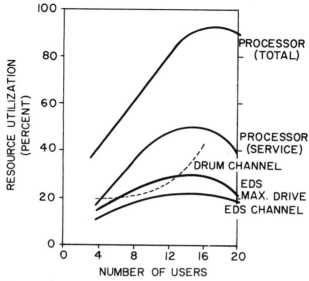

FIG. 3   Resource utilization variation with number of users of a system.

measure. 90- and 95-percent probability response times have characteristics similar to the mean. Frequency distributions are difficult to
compare with each other. Plotting the mean response time to each
message class against the number of users shows that excessive delays
are encountered with an increased number of users. The relative
frequency of these message classes is shown in brackets in Fig. 4.
OS2 consists of creating a new file and copying the contents from
another file into it; OS1 and OS3 are editing messages and short
operating system commands, such as assigning a file to a program.

ALGOL, as referred to in the figures, consists of a successful
compilation and consolidation of a 100-line program. ALGOL FAIL
is an unsuccessful compilation, and runs 1, 2, and 3 are short
program executions.

Figure 5 shows 90 percent probability response times. Such a
mean response time against total CPU utilization shows how futile
overloading the system is. Figure 6 shows the effects of varying
the main store size, while Fig. 7 shows the effect of different CPU
powers. There's an unlimited number of possibilities to investigate.

Figure 8 shows the effects of different workloads on the same
configuration, all at 128 K wsords. Workload 2 uses fewer program
executions than workload 1 uses, and it uses a 32 K word Fortran
compiler. Workload 3 uses only BASIC and JEAN, both interactive

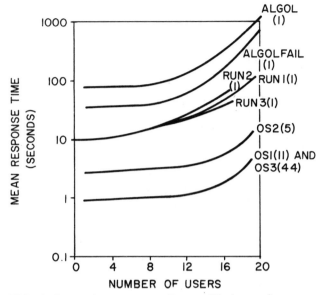

FIG. 4   Increasing response times with increasing complexity of program.

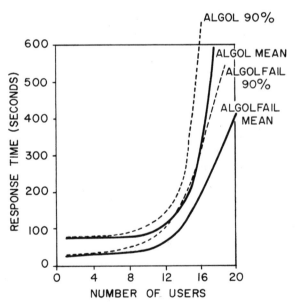

FIG. 5   Increase in mean response time when total
processor utilization rises.

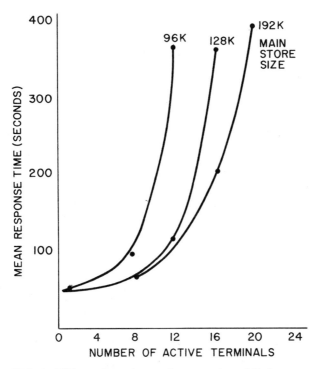

FIG. 6 Effect of varying main store size while keeping workload constant.

compilers with a maximum main store requirement of 9 K words.
Here a response time ratio is plotted against the number of users.
This representation has the advantage that messages with dissimilar
orders of magnitude and resource requirements, and hence response
times, appear on the same scale. Notice that the number of users a
given configuration can support is heavily dependent on the workload characteristics. This is underlined here by the effect of additional main store.

In Fig. 9, note that workload 1 is less dependent on main
store than is workload 2. In fact, from the resource utilizations we
know that it's CPU limited, and you would expect that extra core
wouldn't have too much effect.

From such graphs, the multi-access handling capability of the
system can be determined according to the benchmark criterion.
Possibly this is a response time ratio of 3-to-1 (three times the
response time with one user). This is illustrated in Fig. 8: for
workloads 1 and 2 the system can support 13 users, for workload 3,
20 users. Another criterion might be the maximum resource utiliza-

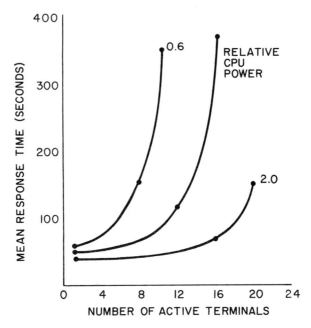

FIG. 7   Machines with different CPU powers compared.

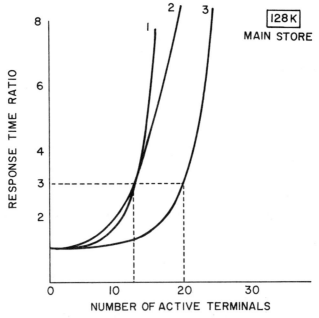

FIG. 8   Effect of varying workload while keeping store size constant at 128 K.

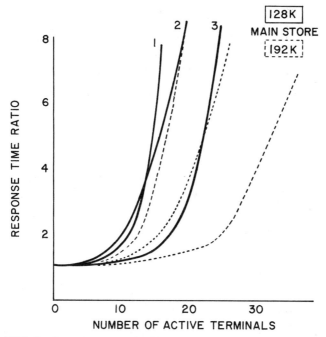

FIG. 9   Combination of effects—increasing core size and different workloads.

tion of 70 to 80 percent on the CPU, 60 to 70 percent on the discs, etc. As the CPU is usually the most costly single item—it still is, and it will be for quite a while, I think—it should be selected first, bearing in mind the spare capacity and enhancement capability to allow for future growth. Having determined the correct CPU, then the rest of the configuration should be balanced. Excess capability in main store or discs should be discarded unless these spare capacities form part of the resilience requirements. An enhancement plan should be prepared and updated throughout the life of the computer system.

To sum up, we would like to underline the following points. Before the implementation of a benchmark is commended, the objectives of the benchmark and the criteria against which the results are to be evaluated must clearly be stated. Benchmarking can consist of both live measurements and predictions. Alternative benchmark implementation techniques should be evaluated and costed for every benchmark. And, finally, benchmarking should be undertaken as a continuous process that involves monitoring the current workload, thereby enabling detailed forward planning to be undertaken and frequently updated.

DISCUSSION

Mr. Blackman (Arthur Andersen): I'm particularly interested in which ranges of equipment this work has been done on, and whether the results will be available to a commercial user.

Dr. Sutcliffe: Most of the work that has been described has been done on the 1900 range. The results are available to our ICL field staff for use with customers and, therefore, should be available in that form to customers.

Dr. Wichmann (NPL): I'd like to point out that from the user's point of view the exerciser, which is extremely convenient in multi-access testing, does have one problem, and that is it's rather difficult for the user to validate that the manufacturers actually perform the tests as stated because it's all done behind the scenes, so to speak.

Dr. Sutcliffe: I'm sorry, what goes on behind the scenes?

Dr. Wichmann: If a multi-access test is done with real live terminals, you can actually see those real live terminals performing the work. For an exerciser, then, there may be no physical evidence of that work being performed when it's actually being done—you can only see some line printer output afterwards.

Mr. Bayley: In fact, it's exactly the same with live people on terminals. We can put a processor there that actually knows what the terminals are going to type and that actually responds. If you want to pull the wool over somebody's eyes, there's always some way of doing so.

Dr. Wichmann: I think it's somewhat more difficult.

Dr. Sutcliffe: You can do a lot of jobs on the terminal, and you can see what object programs are being run and how many terminals are logged on and this sort of thing. This can be done, so I think that what you say can be shown.

Dr. Wichmann: Yes. I'm pointing out that there is a difficulty, at least with some operating systems. The other point I'd like to mention is that we have found that a straightforward method of exercising systems is to use paper tape loops and teletypes. It's easy to arrange and it's something that almost anybody can handle. For instance, we've done tests on our own system this way with essentially only two people doing the work; you don't need a fleet of people. Of course, it isn't typical of typing rates or thinking times that you would get in a real life situation, but from a comparative point of view I don't think it's too bad.

Dr. Sutcliffe: No, that's fair enough, but if you're going to do this thing with 50 or 100 or 1,000 users, it is difficult to organize. I mean, you've got a physical problem of looking after all these terminals and ensuring they work correctly. You can, of course, try and implement user think times as well with that method, perhaps with a *wait* command or something. In that particular case it does affect the system by placing a process that has to be scheduled into the operating system and, therefore, it's not a particularly good method. I suppose you could read yards of tape to simulate the think time as well.

Mr. W. F. Wood (ICL): I'm having difficulty at the moment in squaring what was stated as to a strategy of using an analytic technique based on the results of a hardware investigation with the subsequent emphasis given to a discrete event simulation model. Could you please explain how the three tie in and how they've influenced each other?

Dr. Sutcliffe: Well, yes, I think that we need to be able to present a spectrum of techniques for evaluation exercises. First of all, one would use, as I say, an analytical technique in every case. Then, performance information, which is based on actual measured systems, is worth its weight in gold, but we can't measure the systems of the future and therefore we turn to prediction techniques. They may be based on queuing theory or whatever, and in certain cases it's essential, I believe, to go to simulation modeling, which can incorporate all the interactions together. If we validate the simulation model against actual current systems, then we have much more confidence in the fact that it will predict the effects of future systems. When these become available we must then calibrate the model again and make sure that we have represented things correctly. Just like any other technique, we will constantly improve it.

Unidentified speaker: Were there any surprises that your simulation model revealed that you wouldn't have expected from your earlier analytical models?

Dr. Sutcliffe: Well, yes, in fact I predicted the effects of the increased operating system resource requirements with an increased number of users. Some people said I was wrong. They said that however many users you have, they will level off. In this particular case, we were short of store, as I said earlier, and users had to share the same amount of store, and therefore we got into a main store limited case.

Richard Jones (Harwell): I would like to query the situation where with a certain number of users you reach a saturation point, and your response times start to go sky high. I would suggest in that sort of situation users are going to vary their mode of working. For example, if you know that the response is going to be sluggish, you will take care. Before you type in a line, and before you press *carriage return* or *send* or whatever, you will have a damned good look at that line before you let it go because you know you're not going to get the system back again for a little while. Therefore, what you're going to see is a very substantial change in the user think time. You're going to get a change in the pattern of commands that people will use, and so I would suggest that your figures here are interesting and they're very relevant, but I think that you can probably squeeze more users onto the system than that because of this mechanism.

Dr. Sutcliffe: Certainly increased think times do allow you to put more users on. To my mind you're talking about the saturated case where one resource is limiting the system, and you get long response times. With more main store you find that it's not too critical. What I would hope is that when they're getting a bad response they would log out so we would come down to the saturation point again and everybody will be happy; they'll come back when the load is lower. That's what I'd like people to do.

Mr. Bayly: It's important to know that it's sensible to do your evaluation for worst cases. You don't want to be too optimistic. We're not saying that anybody would rather run that system in this control environment. They obviously don't. All we're trying to show is a spectrum of workload, a spectrum of the number of users, and to show what happens when it does go over the top, and then to try and establish where this point is, this point of instability where a small increase in the number of users can double the response time. One more user might double the response time for all. What I'd like to try and do is to try and find where this point is, the point I call saturation point, which you can define in many ways.

IBM speaker: I'd like to put in a plea for the world to change itself to suit me. I see once again you've been talking about workload all the time, and yet what we have is a graph of a number of users or a number of terminals, which does not constitute a measure of workload. Instead it constitutes a quantity of workload of unknown type, and it seems to me rather like evaluating a batch system against a number of cards that are input to the installation in a day. In one of your graphs you had types, BASIC, JEAN and Fortran, which I'd thought were rather similar in nature. If one takes BASIC as one extreme and at the other extreme a man who could, say, hold a 1906S on his own, doing interactive graphics work for example, that really is an enormous range of workload type which you haven't shown. What I'd like to do is to plead with you and everyone else who presents such graphs to define the actual nature of the workload, and not just a quantity of unknown nature.

Mr. Bayly: The first workload consisted of Algol principally, and indeed the principal component of it was compilations of Algol. The second workload was defined as Fortran with a limited number of runs where the first one had a fair number of runs. The last, the third workload, was defined as the use of interactive compilation systems, rather than batch type compilation systems from a terminal. One could say that if we actually presented all the workloads and defined them in the terms that you want us to define them in, we would be here all afternoon, but we have definitions of each of these workloads and they are absolute definitions.

IBM speaker: It would help if you presented these details so that we could judge for ourselves.

Mr. Bayly: I agree with you, but we can't do everybody's mix. If we do enough of them, and we have enough graphs to cover enough cases, you can at least put yourself between two lines on the graphs, and that's better than not having anything to start with.

IBM speaker: The other point I would say is I think that your workload type covers a very narrow field.

Mr. Bayly: Yes—the ones that we've presented are.

Mr. M. D. P. Fasey (Admiralty Research Laboratory): Arising to some extent out of the last question, I was interested to see your definition of a multi-access system, and it didn't include the one essential item that I felt it should. That is, the computing was done more out of centralized control than any other sort of computing, and hence it's very difficult to know exactly what remote users were doing. Is an up-to-date benchmark the sort of tool to find out whether somebody, if not reinventing the wheel, is reinventing the juggernaut at one of your terminals?

Mr. Bayly: Well, a benchmark certainly isn't the way to find out. If, as suggested, you're using a paper tape loop, for instance, to run a terminal, you can find out what sort of use is actually being made of the system. If your system is a dedicated multi-access system, for instance, it may be appropriate for you to monitor the system by what might be called a benchmark program or a benchmark script, running it every two weeks in the terminal at that particular time and ascertaining, for instance, what your responsiveness is. From that you can actually see whether somebody is inventing the juggernaut by using a crude sampling technique.

Mr. Fasey: So essentially it isn't an up-to-date benchmark, it's a uniformly out of date benchmark that you're using.

Mr. Bayly: I'd like to see the day when we can actually predict what our users are going to do tomorrow morning. Unfortunately, it depends on which side of bed they got out.

Mr. D. J. K. Greggains (Unilever): There are two things: first, an observation regarding our IBM friend's question. I'm sure pigs would fly before he would use your system, but as a heavy user of time sharing, or multi-access if you prefer, I get the impression that everybody is talking about extremely trivial, unsophisticated time-sharing use. He mentioned interactive graphics. I mean, no one yet has talked about this sort of heavy usage. You talk about these programs shown in the graph up on the screen, and yet these seem to more or less ignore things like heavy file access. Your disc accessing can tie up the whole file channel, and yet people don't seem to be thinking of this. The question then really is, how on earth do you find out what is a typical workload for a multi-access system?

I've sent out questionnaires to 20 or 30 heavy users in my own organization. I have also got means of trying to find out what they're doing from the computer bureau side. The question is, they bear virtually no relationship to what the people appear to be doing.

Mr. Bayly: It's always the case. I think, in fact, the reason we've concentrated on aspects such as program development and execution is that that tends to be the most unpredictable part of the multi-access workload. If you have a group of people actually using their terminals for interactive design work, let's say, you have some better control. You don't usually have 30 or 40 people, except in a few CAD centers, and if you have been one of the people approached by a CAD center for use of your machine by them, you will probably have jumped back in fright because the programs are large, the workload's large, but to some extent it's actually defined, and very rigidly defined.

Mr. Greggains: I don't really agree. I'll agree with that specific part of it, but not in general. I would say compilation is one of the most nicely defined things you can do. What is really unpredictable is a large, fairly sophisticated use of programs where the user doesn't know what he's going to do except for his first step, and then the result of his first step is going to lead to a second step, and so on. He has started an absolutely unpredictable chain on interactions. You've no idea what may happen. Data base is an example of this, which, again, no one is talking about, and yet data base is multi-access. We're talking about playing with children's toys at the moment, not using computers as surely they should be used.

Mr. Bayly: Certainly from information retrieval the problems that you state are very real, but I'm afraid that I haven't an immediate solution.

Mr. T. Knowles (GEC Computers Ltd.): I'd like to ask the speakers if they have any views on what role a manufacturer should take in the evaluation of his own equipment in providing data to enable people to predict response times and so on.

Mr. Bayly: Well, in the role of the manufacturer, there are two guiding lights. The first is know your own product, and the second is let the world know what your product is as far as possible.

As to actually enabling people to calculate their own response times, this is quite a difficult task. There isn't a handle you can turn that will churn out the result; what you come out with is some numbers, and you need a great deal of judgment in order to use them. Therefore, it's a skilled operation, and I'd rather not put it in a book, in case people try to misuse it. I think it should be offered as a service, possible through consultancy or possibly from the manufacturer to work with the customers and do the calculations. Together they could sign off those calculations, one could sign off one part and the other sign off the other, and the calculations are signed off by both.

Mr. Knowles: You mentioned that you've done hundreds of runs in order to evaluate your equipment. Do you find this has paid off in the sense that your customers believe the results that you quote?

Mr. Bayly: We have more confidence, that's the important thing. If you've got doubts about your own capability, no wonder the market has doubts.

Dr. Sutcliffe: Yes, we do our best to convince people that the results are accurate. I think they're accurate.

The Design of Synthetic Programs-I

Brian A. Wichmann

National Physical Laboratory

(The views expressed in this paper are those of the author and not
necessarily those of the Laboratory.—*Editor*)

I'm going to talk about one special area of performance
measurement. It's very important to understand that I'm not considering anything more than that highly specialized area, and that is
measuring the processor speed of computers doing scientific work.
What I am concerned with is a sort of naked processor with just
enough core store to run the programs that we're talking about. In
many ways it is a rather artificial situation but, nevertheless, it's an
important figure in quite a few applications, and in any case it's a
useful fact to know about any computer. I shall set the scene and
explain some of the preliminary details as to how we arrived at the
actual synthetic benchmark, but its detailed description will be
handled in the next chapter.

First, I'd like to discuss a number of tools. The first one, and
the most important one from our point of view, is the use of
standard high-level languages. The work that I have been doing is
almost entirely with Algol 60, simply because we use Algol 60 a lot
at NPL. I have been able, as I'll explain later, to obtain a lot of
details about how people use Algol 60. Now Algol has a very
significant advantage—it is machine independent. Algol 60 programs
can be taken from one computer to another, and they do, in general,
produce comparable results. Of course, one does have machine
dependencies, things like the floating point length and so on, that

cannot be entirely removed, but nevertheless a scientific program written in Algol 60 and Fortran can, by and large, be removed around from computer to computer successfully. This means that one has with such a program a machine-independent description of a task that one wants to perform. This is essential for comparison.

The other advantage is that one automatically takes into account the effects of the compiler, the effects of the machine architecture, everything, really, that is involved in the analysis of the processor's speed using high level languages. Now I've obtained quite a lot of statistical information about computers, and I've found out that you can easily smother yourself with data. It is very important, therefore, that one should have some tools at hand to analyze and present the data in a manner that can be easily understood and hopefully not misinterpreted. This is particularly important because often one has to produce a single figure of merit or something that is a little bit absurd, because that's the only thing that the nontechnical staff higher up in the management levels can understand.

Now let us say that we've got machine A and machine B (see Table 1), so as not to cause any problems of commercial confidentiality, and we have two different tasks, which I've put down as time 1 and time 2, giving us a matrix of times. Now here, of course, I've just used two tasks and two machines to illustrate the techniques. In practice one gets a very large number of machines, a very large number of tasks, too much to put into the table, but one can visualize the problem. In this case there is no difficulty in discovering the essential information from that data, namely that machine A is three times as fast as machine B, and task 2 involves quite as much work as task 1.

But, of course, things don't actually turn out like that in practice. In general, we will have a large matrix, T_{ij}, such that

$$T_{ij} \approx S_i \times M_j$$

S_i = time depending on the statement only

M_j = factor for the machine, taken as unity for one machine (arbitrarily)

In fact

$$T_{ij} = S_i \times M_j \times R_{ij}$$

but one would expect each element of that matrix to be a product of a factor that depends upon the complexity of the task and a factor

TABLE 1   Comparison between two
computers

	Machine A	Machine B
Time 1	1	3
Time 2	2	6

Result: Machine A is three times as fast
as B
Time 2 involves twice as much
work as time 1.

that depends upon the speed of the machine. So one has T_{ij}—we have
four of them. That will only be an approximate relationship, so
actually one has the formula on the bottom with equality where the
R_{ij} are numbers that should be approximately equal to 1. Now there
is a standard statistical method of solving that set of equations, the
least squares fitting method. With it you can reach an explicit
solution quite easily. It allows one immediately to obtain factors for
the speeds of the machine on all those different tasks, a sort of
average factor. But the important thing about that average factor is it
doesn't take into account whether one task is more important than
another, so it's not a true performance measure. It's important to
realize that, but it's very handy because often you don't know how
to weight your individual tasks, so a method that doesn't involve
weighting, like this one, is therefore quite convenient.

In Table 2 there is an example of the sort of thing one would
get in practice, but again visualize a much larger matrix if you can,
where we now no longer have an exact fit, and we can't say that
machine A is three times as fast as machine B. If we apply the
mathematical formula I had before, we obtain those as the estimated
times (Table 3), and the deduction is that machine A is now 2.74
times faster than machine B.

Another important aspect is how to get a good graphical
representation of the data that one gets. Now, the technique that I

TABLE 2   Comparison where there is not
an exact fit

	Machine A	Machine B
Statement 1	1	3
Statement 2	2	5

TABLE 3   Estimated times of the same
run done on two computers

	Machine A	Machine B
Statement 1	1.05	2.86
Statement 2	1.91	5.23

Machine A is now 2.74 times faster than
machine B.

have used, which I commend to you, is the use of logarithmic scales
for a start. The classic case is of a well known journal, a weekly
publication, producing on the front page a plot of the supposed
speed of ICL's New Range of computers, and there is a little twiddly
line at the top because they couldn't get the most important high
speed member of that family in on the graph. The result was that it
was entirely useless, whereas if you represent things on a logarithmic
scale you can get the information in a wide range of processor
powers quite happily. Moreover, since improvements in software and
hardware tend to be percentage rather than absolute, it's much easier
to see the effect on a logarithmic scale paper. Figure 1 shows this
clearly.

Here we have a logarithmic scale on the right—that's 1 right
at the bottom, going up to 8. They're covering a factor of 9 in
processor power on that graph. Now each of the vertical scales
represents a different performance measure; in fact, it's a mix. If

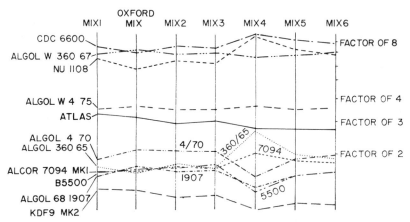

FIG. 1 Comparison between different computers processing different
programs.

there were exact agreement between those scales, we would get
horizontal lines throughout. You can see instantaneously from Fig. 1
that there's something peculiar about mix 4. If you had a table of
figures, which in this case would be 7 by 11 values you would be
inundated with figures, and you wouldn't be able to make sense of
them. You certainly wouldn't spot instantaneously that there was
something funny about mix 4. In this case, what this information
represents is the variation in speed of processors with workload
number 4 looking a bit different.

     Now why is this? Well, we can go back to the basic statistics
on which it's based and discover that mix 4 is odd. It consists of
rather a small number of programs, and therefore is not too reliable a
mix but, moreover, it's very untypical in the use it makes of
mathematical functions. It makes very heavy use of mathematical
functions, and those are calculated with some speed on a 360/65 and
are calculated rather poorly, shall we say, on a 4/70. You will see in
Fig. 1 that they rapidly change over on mix 4.

     In Fig. 2 we have another graph illustrating similar points.
Here we've represented a number of different performance measures.
I'm not going to go into the details of all of them, but here we have a
factor of about 20 in the processor power. Again, you can rapidly
distinguish the various ups and downs, so you tend to ignore the
horizontal lines and look to see where things suddenly change. For
instance, the GAMM measure seems to correlate rather badly with
everything else, and I shall be coming back to that further on.

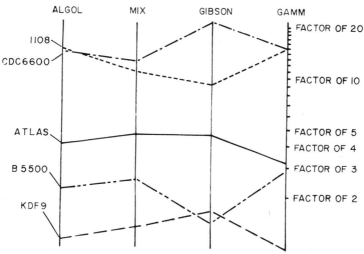

FIG. 2 Comparison of the speed of different computers.

Well, the key to successful performance measurement, therefore, is an adequate statistical description of the workload in the high level language. By that I mean that you must know, for instance, the number of procedure calls you make, the number of array accesses, number of stores, number of fetches, number of conditional jumps, number of jumps, and so on. You must have a really detailed description of the use that you make of the high level language. Now at NPL we run an interpretive Algol 60 system. It is incredibly inefficient, but it's incredibly useful to me. What happens is that an Algol program is translated into a simple stack instruction code, very like the Burroughs 5500 machine code, in fact, and this code is then interpreted very slowly, roughly one instruction every 500 microseconds. Now I could easily patch that interpreter to find out how often each of the 120 or so different instruction types have been used. Now each one of those instruction types corresponds to a particular source language feature, a semantic feature of Algol 60. So I can relate it directly to the use made of features in Algol 60, in a way that you couldn't do with an ordinary machine code compiler.

With this patch I was able to collect statistics from nearly 1,000 programs at NPL and also, as a check, at Oxford University. I found there was virtually no difference between the programs at Oxford University and those at NPL. Before I had this statistical information, I already had the times, in microseconds, taken for 42 basic statements written in Algol 60. I was able to analyze this information, of course, using the method that I pointed out with the least squares fitting to give me a sort of unweighted measure of performance. However, it was quite clear that some features of Algol 60 were used a lot more heavily than others and, therefore, I needed to weight those statements to produce a proper mix. I was able to do this quite easily and produce the statement mix, but there was a significant drawback of the program at that stage. The basic statements were simply written inside a loop, and an optimizing compiler, for example a Fortran H2 compiler, would take those statements completely out of the loop and defeat the whole object of the exercise. So it's clear that if one was to extend the work to Fortran, or indeed extend it to optimizing Algol 60 compilers, it would be necessary to devise a much more sophisticated program to measure CPU performance. This is just what Mr. Curnow has done.

Before we go on to describe this program, I would like to give you a few examples of the bizarre things that can happen if you don't base a processor test on a proper statistical sampling method. I have a little test called Ackermann's Function, which is the sort of thing that academics would like to play with. In other words, it doesn't do anything of any use whatsoever, but it gives you some interesting results! What it does, in fact, is to calculate a function recursively in a rather nasty manner designed to check whether or not procedure calls can be called rapidly; in other words, it just calls procedures. Very few people spend all their time calling procedures, and I could convert the times that I got to the number of instructions executed, and this is what I've plotted again on a logarithmic scale (see Fig. 3). There's absolutely no reason why any compiler for Algol 60, at least, should take more than about 100 instructions per call on this particular test, so I won't comment on the ones that are above that line. Suppose the KDF9 compiler—this is the true compiler, not the interpreter—is quite respectable in this respect (the Algol W compiler does a bit better). You can code the entire thing in the machine code, and on the KDF9 this involves about 18 instructions. You can, for instance, write the program in Coral 66 on a Modular One where it's performed in about 15 instructions.

In other words, one should be aiming at that sort of performance, but one really does require a certain degree of hardware systems. For instance, on say a machine like a PDP-11 you can do it quite well because you have stacking instructions that allow you to generate quite reasonable code. So although there are problems on conventional hardware where you might go up to say 100 instructions, especially if you do a lot of checking, really you

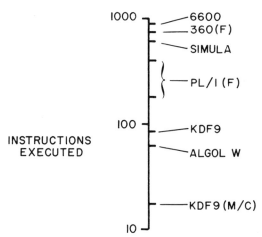

FIG. 3   Procedure call speeds of various computers.

should be able to do this in about 15 instructions. As a sideline, for instance, I might add that on a System 4 machine at Edinburgh there is a language called Imp that effectively encompasses Algol 60 in all practical applications. They can do Ackermann in 11.5 instructions, which rather contrasts with, shall we say, a 360F compiler for exactly the same instruction code.

Take another example (see Fig. 4). This is GAMM. Now perhaps I ought to explain what GAMM is. GAMM is a benchmark that is functionally described in English, or I should say German. What you have to do is do a number of simple numerical loops, things like multiplying two vectors, adding two vectors, doing a square root by Newton's Method, polynomial loop, finding a maximum of a vector, and so on. You can, since it is an English style of description, code this up in any language you like, or in machine code. In Fig. 4 all the languages were Algol 60, unless another language is mentioned. That second line is KDF9 machine code. The trouble with these loops, and what makes them so unrepresentative, is that they are extremely simple and only involve one dimensional array accessing in Algol 60. This means that any optimizing compiler can do a really superb job on these loops, and so they really are very untypical. If you coded the machine code, where you can often make use of special loop control instructions, you find that what this GAMM approach measures is the floating point times and virtually

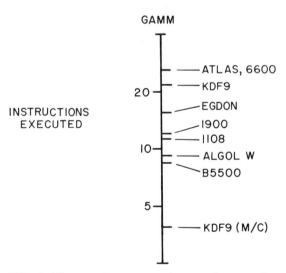

FIG. 4   How various computers perform under GAMM assessment.

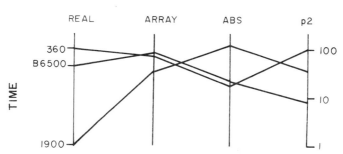

FIG. 5   Comparison of computer speeds when carrying out standard routines.

nothing else. In Algol 60 without successive optimization, as with most Algol compilers, you're only measuring how rapidly you can fetch one dimensional array elements and how rapidly you can do loop control. Now those are very one-sided tests, and you can't really expect it to correlate very highly with a general measure, like our synthetic benchmark.

Figure 5 is another example of the same phenomenon, the phenomenon of the wide variation that one gets. In my basic statements—I've chosen four of them (left to right in the figure)—I am declaring an element in a block *real x*; declaring an array in a block; *begin real x*; *end* the call of the standard function *abs* giving the absolute value of an argument and the call of a procedure *p2*. Well, if one takes out the effect of basic processor speed of the machine, one can plot a residual variation, as in Fig. 5. This shows the very wide variation of order 100 to 1 you get in different systems. Let me describe a few of the idiosyncrasies. The reason why *real x* is so good (good is at the bottom, by the way) on the 1900 is that it is generating no code whatsoever, so that's really what this logarithmic paper should be used to show—singularity. It's a bit difficult to explain that adequately; I'm afraid I drew it to a time of roughly half an instruction time. Well, for instance, *abs* takes a long time on the 1900, and that is because it uses a standard procedure-calling mechanism, rather than handling it as open code as is done, for instance, on the Burroughs 6500. The array declaration, for instance, is appalling on both the 360 and 6500. The basic reason for that is both of them involve supervisor activities. On the 360 it is quite unnecessary; on the 6500 it's a feature of the operating system. That doesn't matter from the point of view of overall performance because array declarations are sufficiently rare for that not to be

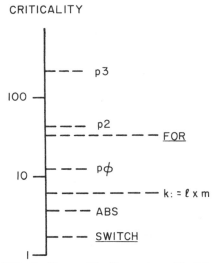

FIG. 6   How criticality varies with different functions.

embarrassing. Consider, for instance, a procedure call; it is extremely good on the Burroughs 6500, that's really no surprise, the hardware does it all for you. On the other hand, a procedure call on the 360, level F compiler, that is, is really pretty terrible, and the reason for that is basically poor implementation.

Now you can define something else. You can define *criticality* as

Criticality = (time in function) $\times$ (variation in performance)

which is, in a nutshell, the length of time you take to do certain things; the measure of how often you call procedures, for instance, multiplied by the variation that you typically get in performance with one system to another. This means the statements with high criticality are the ones that the compiler writer ought to spend a long time on because substantial improvements in performance are possible. If you display criticality you get this sort of table (see Fig. 6), again a logarithmic scale. The call of procedures turns out to be very critical in Algol, but something like a switch or an array declaration, which I haven't actually shown, really hardly matters at all because it just isn't used enough, even though there is a wide variation in its performance.

I think that sets the scene now, and I think you will appreciate the importance of using statistical information on the use of Algol 60 to construct a benchmark.

The Design of Synthetic Programs-II

Harry J. Curnow

Central Computer Agency

As Dr. Wichmann has said, he had gathered a large number of statistics on the use of the intermediate code, which I intend to call *Whetstone Code*. The idea seemed reasonable on my part. Rather than take 42 separate timings, why not roll the whole lot into one program and take a single time? You don't get as much detailed information about the implementation, but you do get an overall speed figure. When I actually did roll his statements into one and translated them into Fortran, then put them through an optimizing compiler, they largely disappeared. So I had to think again.

In the first place the program had to be simple enough to be able to transfer it from one machine to another and translate it into different languages without too much difficulty. Also, it had to be capable of being translated by hand into the Whetstone Intermediate Code with the aid of the book (Randell & Russell, 1964). I had to calculate the frequencies of the different instructions in the program and then match them up in some way to the workload statistics that had been gathered. Quite apart from the effect of throwing out unused code, optimizing compilers also can make a simple program run at an untypically high speed by using fast registers as temporary data stores and various other tricks like that. So the program had to be complex enough to be typical when presented to an intelligent compiler, either an automatic or a human compiler. It becomes a human compiler in the case of a machine that doesn't exist, and that seems to be a popular sort of machine to think about these days.

The best thing to do seemed to be to make sure that the program couldn't be logically optimized, by which I mean chunks being thrown away and so on. I hoped that by writing code that looked natural—in other words, the sort of code that I write, or wrote in the days when I wrote code—I would get somewhere near the right use for fast registers and other hardware features. Then we could say that would be a measure of well-written code. Obviously we'd avoid language peculiarities because we wanted to translate it into other languages. So, modular programming being all the rage, although I didn't know it at the time, the thing seemed to be to have a number of modules of different types using different language features, each of them in a FOR loop. Each module would then have to represent a genuine calculation so that the machine genuinely had to do it, preferably producing a number of different results each time around. One of the problems is that the time taken to do something depends on the actual values of the numbers being processed, so it's a good idea to stir those up a bit. On the other hand, it had to go on more or less indefinitely because to measure a really fast machine you need a fair chunk of computing to get an accurate timing, especially if you're using a stop watch. But we didn't want it to go and overflow numerically or do something else as a result of a large number of repeated calculations. Then, having got the modules, the idea was to adjust the number of repetitions so that the overall statistics of the benchmark program, in terms of the Whetstone Intermediate Code, would match the instruction frequencies that Dr. Wichmann had analyzed.

It seemed important that one should consider the method of fitting the benchmark program to the analysis. One should cover as many instructions as possible, while to keep things nice one should keep down the number of modules, if possible. The obvious thing to do is to minimize the root mean square difference between the instruction frequencies in the benchmark and in the analysis. A refinement of that could be to weight the instructions according to their relative importance. In the Whetstone Code there are some instructions that are fairly simple and correspond approximately to a single machine code instruction. There are one or two big jumbo ones, like sine and cosine, that are single Whetstone Code instructions but call in, on interpretation, a large chunk of actually executed code. Then the strategy was to redesign the modules until a good fit could be obtained. The text of the program is given in Appendix C.

Module number 5 in Appendix C has got lost on the way. We obviously needed, as I said, some genuine calculations capable of going on indefinitely without overflowing, so I looked at a set of four statements in Algol which form module 1 in their simplest form in the eventual program. They look like a set of four simultaneous equations but, of course, being machine code, they're not, although it's possible to analyze them in a similar way to a set of simultaneous equations. Provided t is either ½ or just less than ½, for fun, any starting values of $x1$, $x2$, $x3$, and $x4$ lead to a stable series of calculations. I made an arbitrary choice of t of .499975, and as an arbitrary starting point $x1$ is 1 and $x2 = x3 = x4 = -1$. Then that gave me three modules because in module 1 the xs are just simple variables. In module 2 they are references to elements of an array, and in module 3 they are actually references to elements of an array that is a parameter of a procedure pa shown on the first page of the Appendix. There is a programmed loop in pa so that it goes around six times for each procedure call. This was part of the adjustment of the design of the module to give it a good overall fit. Then I had another couple of almost stationary transformations in module 7 and module 11. In number 7, if you start off with the premises that $x = y$ and $t2 = 2$, given the trigonometric relationships shown, it means that x and y are almost the same as at the beginning. They just vary slowly each time around, and it's all cunningly designed so that, although it looks as though $x + y$ is a common expression that could be carried forward, it isn't. This is because the first statement upsets x and the second statement upsets y when you go around again. It really does have to do all the sines and cosines. Another similar thing that occurs in module 11 is where it does a rather elementary thing with square roots, exponentials, and logarithms.

I was forced into these rather complex expressions because of a general shortage of store instructions in the analysis, which means that the average sort of statement is a fairly complex one. Evidently the programmers at NPL and Oxford University write rather more complex code than the programmers at Stanford (Knuth, 1971).

Then we had to have some jumps, so module 4 has a bit of a fire cracker that plays around with the value of j. It is so designed that each time around when each of the conditions is either true or false it is the opposite of what it was the previous time around. This seemed a good idea at the time, but it's recently been pointed out that certain complicated machines remember which way a branch went the last time and expect to find it going the same way each time. Certain pipeline machines might find that module a bit more awkward than it really should be, to be typical, but I didn't know about those things at that time.

Then we had to have some integer arithmetic, so that went into module 6 together with an array reference with a variable subscript. We wanted a procedure with various sorts of parameters, so I produced $p3$ in module 8, and this just does a bit of arithmetic with three parameters. I was short of procedure calls, but not parameters, so I had to have a parameterless procedure $p0$, which included a chunk of code, and it is called from module 9. It simply circulates some values in an array of references with apparently variable subscripts—they don't actually vary, but it would be a jolly good compiler that could actually spot that fact. Module number 10 was just a bit more integer arithmetic.

I'm presenting this as a single pass operation, but it was an iterative process and it went around a number of times. The next step was to fit the modules to the statistics using, first of all, a standard least squares method. I fitted 25 values over the 10 modules, and those, by hook or crook, represented about 95 percent of the instructions executed in the analysis. By adjustment of the design of the modules a fairly good fit was eventually obtained, first using the standard least squares method, which had the unfortunate tendency of producing some negative values for the ns that control the loops and that, even these days, would be a bit difficult to implement. So I had to modify the fitting method using a direct search method, which is more of a trial-and-error thing, where the range of parameters was constrained to be positive. The method is actually potentially more powerful because it could deal with a nonlinear situation where there were more, as it were, products of parameters controlling some of the things. I didn't, however, get around to that degree of sophistication.

Also I weighted the instructions so that more attention was paid to fitting the important ones by taking some of the results that Dr. Wichmann had obtained on a large number of machines for his statements, and going back from them to the Whetstone Code Instructions. This procedure gave an approximation to the average times for the execution of individual Whetstone Instructions that actually would, in terms of an average sort of machine scale, approximate to an Atlas in power. That's all quite arbitrary though.

With a weighted root mean square measure and using the direct search minimization, modules 1 and 10 were actually thrown out and the remaining eight modules gave a weighted *rms* deviation over the 25 instructions of 15 percent, which seemed quite reasonable. The total nominal time on the average Atlas was 5.93 seconds for the benchmark, compared with 6.08 for the analysis. The total instruction count was 963,000, compared with the target of 1 million. So then the whole program was thrown together, as it is in Appendix C, with i as the controlling parameter. It enables one to adjust the total weight. If you scale the elapsed time to the value of $i = 10$, that corresponds to the execution of one million Whetstone Instructions, if you translated it into Whetstone Instructions. I left modules 1 and 10 in because it's often interesting to look at the object code produced by different statements, particularly comparing 1 and 2. So, by going around that loop a few times the fit was obtained as described.

Well, if you've got a benchmark, I suppose the best thing to do is to run it on some machines and see what happens. The results are given in Fig. 1. The first machine happened to be an IBM 360/65, for no particular reason, and on this machine there are a number of compilers and a number of languages. In Algol there was the F compiler, on Fortran the G and H compilers, which I think are fairly well known as being sort of standard and optimizing. In PL/1 there's an F compiler, an older standard one, and there's also a new PL/1 optimizing compiler. It is possible to represent reals and integers in

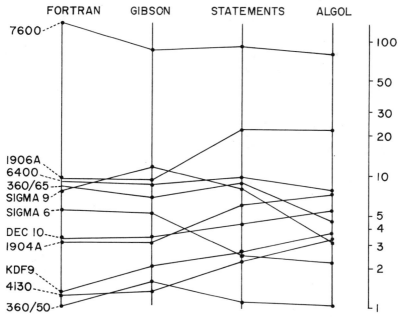

FIG. 1   Comparison of 11 computers carrying out 4 different benchmark programs.

different ways. Reals can either be 6 or 14 hexadecimal floating point, integers either 15 or 31 bit binaries, so I arbitrarily chose 9 decimal (see Table 1). PL/1 is almost the same as Algol, when looked at from the point of view of this program.

Fortran was more or less a straight translation, but I didn't go for an exactly equivalent program, I went for what people would use most of the time. In other words, I used straightforward DO loops, although the formal definition is slightly different. I just put in my own little trap to stop it going through when the n was nought. So we just perm everything on the machine and get a table of execution speeds (see Table 1). The best point to start is probably Fortran G with the standard short precision real and the standard integer representation. Speed measured was 430,000 Whetstone Instructions per second equivalent. The optimizing compiler (H) yields two speeds, one obtained without optimization (OPT is set = 0) and the other with optimization (OPT is set = 2). At this point one should look at one of the design aims of the program, and that was it couldn't be optimized logically. Looking at the object code here, it is actually doing everything in the H case, but it's making better use of the fast registers. It's actually executing, and the main effect is that it just executes fewer machine code instructions, which seems to be a legitimate ploy on the part of the machine. One can also compare Fortran G and H when you use double precision 14 hexadecimal.

The slowdown on double precision in terms of execution time is much the same in Algol and PL/1 as in the Fortran cases. Algol release one, dated July 1967 and never touched since, as far as I know, is rather slow in execution speed, but I guess it's doing a fair amount of checking on parameters and arrays and things during execution. Fortran is very much a case of screw-down-the-safety-valve-and-let-her-rip, you know. Going from G down in Table 1, half-word integers are actually slower than whole-word integers on

TABLE 1   A comparison of IBM 360/65 execution speeds

Representations		Algol	Fortran			PL/1	
Real	Integer	F	G	H		F	OPT
6 Hex	31 Bin	72	430	409 521		372	443
14 Hex	31 Bin	65	321	421		302	336
6 Hex	9 Dec	—	—	—		163	262
6 Hex	15 Bin	—	370	—		—	—

Note: Speeds in 1000's of Whetstone Instructions per second.

this size of machine; that might, of course, be different in a different part of the machine range; I don't know. Here the old PL/1 compiler was obviously not as good as Fortran when measured by this program. All my remarks are related to measurements by this program; I don't wish (at this stage, at any rate—maybe not for a few years) to convert these into absolute statements about the quality of any particular program product. These are just the numbers that I got when I ran this program on this machine. If you happen, by some mishap of not understanding PL/1 too well, to end up with packed decimals for your integers, PL/1F is rather badly stricken because it tends to use a lot of subroutines for the necessary conversions—the optimizer is rather better there. Looked at again, the optimizing compiler in PL/1 nowadays gives very comparable speeds with Fortran G.

Now I've made a number of statements there about the relative capacities of the compilers and the different things, on a fairly sound basis of ignorance about these matters, to illustrate the sorts of conclusions that can be drawn from this benchmark. The problem is to validate the thing. The only way of validating it is to take those 949 programs and shove them through those compilers and see what happens, and it just isn't on. Maybe the only thing to do is to make some provocative statements like this, and see if other people agree that those figures look like reasonably typical figures.

The next machine, featured in Table 2, with some sort of idea of fairness I suppose, was a 1904A from ICL. This also happened to be lying around at hand, and here we were limited to Algol and Fortran. For Fortran there were two compilers, popularly known as XFAT and XFEW. There are two precisions for the reals which are in 37-bit binary floating point, and double precision is, I think, 74-bit binary floating point. The particular 4A had hardware floating point but, of course, not hardware double precision. Bearing in mind the difference in these precisions from those of the other machine makes the comparison a bit difficult, if not invidious. Again, the figures are to the same notional scale of thousands of Whetstone Instruction equivalents.

We have a jolly thing on ICL called TRACE that enables you to adjust the pressure on the safety valve. With TRACE 0 you screw it right down and let everything go, and again the XFEW optimizer is doing its job by basically generating fewer instructions, by being more intelligent about it, and using its limited resources on the machine. Algol is—well, it's in there fighting. If you put the TRACE 1 on, you get various combinations of safety valves, which in fact are different between Fortran and Algol, to make life more difficult, but

TABLE 2   Comparison of ICL 1904A execution speeds

	Algol	Fortran			
	XALT	XFAT		XFEW	
Trace level	Single	Single	Double	Single	Double
0	125	159	20.8	192	21
1	58	91	19.2	100	19
2	52	17	9.4	59	17.5
3	55	—	—	—	—

Note: Speeds in 1000's of Whetstone Instructions per second.

by TRACE 2 they are more or less the same. They are checking for overflow pretty frequently, and if anything goes wrong you get a sensible traceback of where you were in the program. Double precision, as I said, is not hardware and therefore is rather slow. If you take away the hardware single-precision floating point, then I think the speed goes down to about 9 thousand.

So, again, one is able to make a few deductions about the speed of the machine, the speed of different compiler options, that sort of thing. Again, in all honesty, doing this exercise has been my main education in the internal workings of computers, and therefore any observations I make should be treated with due caution. It would be interesting, though, to know what people think of this sort of performance measurements.

Table 2 was prepared by Dr. Wichmann by the methods he has already described, and *Fortran* means my benchmark program in Fortran and *Algol* means my benchmark program in Algol, but *Statements* means his statement mix, and *Gibson* means a Gibson Mix of instruction speeds. When worked out by his methods, it looks as though my Fortran program correlates quite well with the Gibson Mix which, considering the rather devious routes by which they were derived, perhaps means something. This is especially satisfying when you consider that Gibson is based on programs analyzed in the United States by IBM and the Fortran program was translated from Algol through the Whetstone Interpretive Code from a load of different programmers programming at NPL and at Oxford University, some years ago. If we get a correlation like that, perhaps it means something; I don't know.

I will just briefly summarize some thoughts about what we may have here. The program is intended to be a model of the original analyzed programs, the idea being that by running it on a new type of machine you may learn something about the performance of the machine in terms of what it would have had if you'd run the original load of programs. As I said, we can't validate that directly, so it's a matter for other people to judge whether they think this measure is a useful one or not. Assuming that it is, there are a number of limitations which, as with all these methods of measurement, must be borne in mind. I would say that it's probably a typical program in terms of the mixture of machine code functions that it exercises, and in the sort of sequence in which they occur. For instance, I have analyzed the code from the 1904A and find that branch instructions occur in a percentage of around 19 percent. By the way, may I say that I am a lazy mathematician, and I tend to let other people do their own roundings in the way they like to do it, so I do occasionally produce apparently accurate-looking figures, but I don't believe them any more than anybody else.

It does go around loops rather a lot of times per loop because of the way it was written. It might have been better to go the minimum number of times around each loop, and put the whole thing into a calculated loop. As I said, I made some effort to stir up the values of the operands of the arithmetic instructions, so they may not be untypical. The standard function library in the high-level language system is attacked fairly typically, but obviously the input/output is not intended to be typical. The output is only put there to make quite sure that the computer actually does have to do something, like produce some numbers. There is no such thing as a completely CPU-bound job because an intelligent machine would just not do it.

This program is getting less typical by the hour because people will keep inventing types of computers so much more complicated that nobody really knows what is typical for them. The data area that it uses is very small, so it represents programs that use small data areas. This is now much more significant with multi-level storage systems. The Fortran H compiler manages to get the whole of module 4 into general purpose registers without a single store access. That is not typical, it's just part of the thing. The whole thing is worked so that if any particular part of it goes wrong, then that only represents a small part of the program, so, provided that doesn't happen too many times, you may still be in business.

With these various types of buffered, slaved, or virtual-store machines, all we can say is that it's untypical. I have produced a modified version that accesses a larger area of store, but that's an arbitrary sort of exercise, so it's marginally less untypical. Obviously we can't hope to produce a benchmark program or any other sort of performance measurement that will remain valid for any conceivable machine. The performance of new machines is determined by factors that we just do not know now and will only be able to determine accurately when we have machines of that type running for some time so that we can learn what the user workload characteristics are internally. Still, despite all these limitations, maybe this program has some value, particularly for smaller machines which, in general, are simpler machines and do behave in a reasonably sequential fashion. It provides a measure of computer speeds and a similar level of usefulness to the Gibson Mix, but it does take account of actual compilers and software in the way they manage to put the machine to use. So it does mean that we can look at different compilers and options in evaluating a machine.

Another possible application would be in the CPU load component of a more comprehensive total-load benchmark as applied to a complete system, or as one of the dots on Mr. Berners-Lee's matrix of machine-dependent to independent factors. In any case, I hope that maybe the general principles that I've worked on in setting this up may suggest ways of proceeding in a rather difficult situation.

DISCUSSION

Unidentified speaker: I wonder if I could ask Mr. Curnow to expand on one of the more recent statements he made. I'm not clear as to how changes in machine technology are going to affect the validity of this benchmark because, as I understand from his talk, the benchmark was derived from an analysis of problem programs. It would seem that the problem programs would stay constant; simply the way that they were solved by particular computers would alter. The problems themselves stay the same and valid, surely?

Mr. Curnow: When I said computer technology—maybe I should have said computer architecture—that doesn't mean changing from valves to transistors. The point is that the characteristics that determine the performance of the machine are characteristics that do not appear in the analysis because, among other things, they were irrelevant on the machine that was then running. Therefore, one cannot construct a model program that is correct from the point of view of those characteristics. We can only say that the program looks right at the Whetstone Intermediate Code level and, since most machines work through that sort of interface, it will probably be right for a large number of machines. It will be particularly right, maybe, for machines in which that sort of code is close to the machine code. It will not be so good on machines for which that sort of code is far away from the machine code.

If you run this program on a 370 machine with a cache store, then you will find that the entire program will get inside the cache. Therefore it will run untypically fast. Certainly there are quite a few programs that will stay within the cache; after all, if that were not true it wouldn't be worth having, but the data area it works on is very small. We haven't any information about the size of the data areas; that information isn't available, unfortunately, so that particular parameter hasn't been adjusted adequately, and if you run this program on a 370 machine, you have to look at the figures with caution. That's the best way of putting it, I think. On the other hand, if you, say, run this program on a Burroughs 6700, whose code corresponds very closely indeed to the Whetstone Interpretive Code, I would expect that the figure you would get for CPU performance of that machine would correspond very closely to what we would discover on the benchmark.

Eric Foxley (Nottingham University): Your Fortran version of the benchmark seems to me to have rather dubious parentage in that it's an analysis of Algol programs giving an Algol mix translated into Fortran. I don't really see why that should necessarily represent a typical mix of Fortran instructions. Have you done any work seeing whether this is the case or how distorted it is? Similarly, I would have thought that the PL/1 translation needs some comparison with actual PL/1 usage before it becomes worthwhile as a benchmark. And lastly, can this be expanded to general job loads because in our case of large computer services, things like job overheads are as important to us as the speed of running compiled code?

Mr. Curnow: No, I haven't really done any serious study of Fortran or PL/1 real programs apart from actually writing a few Fortran ones myself and reading a paper on Fortran statistics. From the point of view of the people at NPL, who are not too dissimilar from myself, I would say that the features that they would have used, if they had been using Fortran, would have been very much like the ones they were using when they were using Algol. That's purely a personal sort of feeling. Similarly with PL/1; there we have a language that is a bit more of everything to everybody. This can only pretend to be represented doing this type of work.

Unidentified speaker: I wanted really to ask two questions. First of all, was your initial analysis of these some 1,000 programs from Oxford and yourself and NPL a static analysis of just the source code, or was it a dynamic analysis of the usage of language features while the programs were actually running? The second question, was the yardstick in the presentation of your results in terms of Whetstone or equivalent Whetstone Instructions? Would it not be more useful to designers of systems, who are wondering what are the penalties for using a high level language rather than machine code, to have produced absolute times for the running of these benchmarks? These would take account, not only of the inefficiencies of the high level language compiler, but also of the actual times of execution of instructions in the machine itself. In other words, a fast machine will always produce a better end result in absolute terms.

Dr. Wichmann: Let me take some of those points. Can I make a short commercial? There is a reference (Wichmann, 1973) to a publication that does contain all of the information that we collected at NPL. All of this work essentially has been based on the dynamic use of Algol 60 features, but there is in that book details about static usage as well, unfortunately from a different sample of programs, so beware.

Now your second point—you can convert. That's quite easy; you can convert those times to absolute times if you wish, but one does tend to deal in terms of the number of instructions it takes to do something rather than the absolute time. This is best illustrated perhaps with a range of machines like the 360 or 370. What remains constant is the number of instructions you execute to do the task, but the time can vary by a factor of 100, you see, so in many cases the number of instructions executed is more useful.

Mr. Curnow: Can I make one point quite clear? The thing quoted in my diagrams is speed in Whetstone Instructions per real second, so you can take a million Whetstone Units as a standard chunk of workload and from that you can either express it as a speed or as a time to execute that. It's done that way because, given a particular machine, you can investigate the relationship between the average Whetstone Instruction and the average machine code instruction. For the 360 machine it seems to be approximately 1.3 to 1.4 machine codes per Whetstone. For an ICL machine it's about 1.6 to 2, depending on which compiler and which language, that sort of thing. These are very approximate figures just quoted off the top of my head.

Mr. Greggains (Unilever): I feel a little bit unhappy at the moment because there's a large class of user who seems to be being ignored. Benchmarking seems to be becoming almost an end in itself, I'm beginning to think. There's a language called *Cobol* which we use sometimes.

There's something called *file handling* which you've just tried to ignore. There are channel utilizations. Some of these benchmarks seem to be very applicable to a university or academic job shop, but they seem to be losing touch with a commercial user who still buys a lot more computers than the universities, who usually get them cheap anyway. Can you offer any help to us in the commercial environment where we have very real problems of getting the payroll out? Because I want my pay slip on Friday or at the end of the month, not based on whether I can get through my regression analysis of 5,000 points on a sales graph, but the rather different style of work altogether of a commercial environment, rather than the academic job shop environment.

Dr. Wichmann: I'm very sensitive to your criticism because it has been made several times, but I issue a challenge to you. The reason why I have been able to do this work is because I've been able to get out statistics on the use made of Algol 60; everything has stemmed from that. Now, if you can provide me with the hooks and the figures whereby I can find out what 1,000 different Cobol programs do, then one can go to town and produce something. But a word of warning: Cobol unfortunately varies from machine to machine. It isn't as machine independent, for instance, as Algol 60. Moreover, good Cobol programmers know how Cobol has got to be mapped in machine code on their machine, and they design their data formats appropriately. This means you can be in the somewhat invidious situation where you have an apparently machine-independent Cobol program, and you transcribe it to another machine, where all hell is let loose because things don't fit nicely, and you get a factor-of-two explosion. What I'm saying is that there are a lot of deep technical problems in tackling this, but the real problem, the first problem, really, is to get adequate statistical information.

Mr. Greggains: But, in fact, in that answer you've just defined why I want to do it. It's because of these vast differences that it's so desperately important to do it.

Dr. Wichmann: I agree. Well, you know, give us the information or the means of getting it. I haven't got Cobol on my machine, and all the people I work with don't program in Cobol, so I've really no means of coming to grips with the problem, although I'd welcome the opportunity to do so.

Mr. Berners-Lee: This area is a difficult one, although some attempts have been made. Three or four years ago now, when we were talking to an American manufacturer about this, they produced a mix that had been based on hand analysis of a large sample of Cobol programs. Another manufacturer in France has got consultants who have got out a Cobol mix. When we looked at these Cobol mixes we found they were roughly a third actual arithmetic, a third string moves, and a third string comparisons. When we compared them, there were interesting differences that had quite a substantial effect on their performance. For example, it turns out to be quite important to get the average length of the strings which are being moved. This is one of the things that do differ between different machine architectures. I quite agree that altogether too little work has been done in this area, and progress has got to take place in the way in which Brian Wichmann has described.

Unidentified speaker (Rank Xerox): I'd just like to draw attention to the caution in using synthetic programs and, if we look at the graph you produced on comparative powers of machines, you will find that a 4130 is slightly more powerful than a Sigma 6 for the Algol synthetic program.

Mr. Curnow: It was a GT 4130! It had a faster core store; it was a 750 *ns* core store, in fact.

Previous speaker: All right. Perhaps, then, this graph doesn't illustrate my point, but previous graphs have done with comparisons between the Sigma 6 and the 4130. We have found that in running typical Algol programs, people have produced significantly better results. I found this recently on a benchmark I did. I think our last three benchmarks showed this as well, and were consistent in predicting better performance, in using these typical Algol programs, and in using the synthetic Algol program.

Dr. Wichmann: Well it all depends what you mean by typical, doesn't it? I mean, it's very easy, if you know what you're doing, to get a program to run slower, shall we say, on a CDC 6600 than on a KDF9. Any machines that vary by a factor of two in performance, by doing the right things you can make them do whatever you like. The point is that this benchmark is based on statistics from 1,000 programs, and we believe that those 1,000 programs, as submitted to the 4130 and the Sigma 6, would overall show that pattern.

Previous speaker: Yes, I think now that, although the last three benchmarks we've done must have covered 50-100 programs, there is still a significant difference.

Dr. Wichmann: Yes, well, you've still got another factor of 10 to go.

Second Day Morning Chairman Philip J. Kiviat (Federal Computer Performance Evaluation and Simulation Center, Washington, D.C.): No, I don't think that's even the point. The point is that your 1,000 programs are in NPL and his 100 are someplace else. The real question lies in what the difference is between the two usages in some broad sense, and that doesn't come out here at all.

Dr. Wichmann: Yes, perhaps I ought to point something else out. I believe there are moves to revise the Algol compiler and therefore, of course, things could change fairly radically, and you can see roughly how they could change. Other things being equal, if you were, for instance, completely rewriting an Algol compiler, one might reasonably expect the graphs for the Sigma 9 and the Sigma 6 to go straight across. Now you can translate that quite rapidly in that diagram into genuine savings.

Mr. Jones (Harwell): Just a brief observation. In our particular environment we are a darn sight more worried about how fast the compiler runs than how fast the code it produces runs.

Dr. Wichmann: Yes, well I have collected quite a lot of information about compiled times in the course of running these programs, and so has Harry Curnow. The difficulty is to make sense of the figures you get. Operating systems are not universally helpful in this respect. You get into this horrible area of peripheral transfers, which seems to foul everything up. They should be done away with! You know, the length of time a program takes to compile does typically depend upon what else is in the machine. Now there's usually some accounting numbers produced, but what they actually mean is difficult to understand—you have to be in the master class to interpret those correctly. Moreover, the method of interpretation varies from operating system to operating system, and so you rapidly find that to analyze compile times you are, in fact, analyzing an operation system. Therefore, we haven't been able to produce any really sensible figures in this area.

Unidentified speaker (IBM): I find that the fascinating factor, particularly in the business where you are comparing use of packed decimal for scientific work; it is a little unusual against more conventional type of data. It's only a slight shame that you weren't able to use a more modern Algol compiler. But there are a couple of points that I wanted to make. One was on the whole business of architecture, and that is to say this about the hit rate in the cache. You could dynamically trace, and hence work out, what the effect of a cache would be. After all, that's how the cache is designed and verified in the first instance. But with the design on the 370s or on the large 360s the cache hit rate doesn't vary very much with the type of program. This is so, even with commercial sorts, because a sort is a particularly bad thing for the cache, but it's still got a very high hit rate. You're much more likely to hit variability in run time with other parameters such as the amount of real storage in a virtual storage system, and that could have very significant effects if you had an 8 megabyte program in an 8 K machine. It could take quite a long time to run. But I think more important even than the machine architecture is what you might call the software architecture because both hardware and software are designed according to various factors, such as sequentiality factors in program execution and data reference. These are difficult to evaluate, and the H compiler is a good example where you can easily get a halving in a run time. Just the sort of thing that you should not be experiencing on the cache. If you are able to optimize a particular code, and obviously if you put together a program synthetically, it's a little difficult to aver that the result is an average sort of program.

The second point is: my experience in running hardware monitors in scientific installations is that they're as I/O bound as hell, and that's the same experience that I get elsewhere, whereas commercial installations are very often CPU bound. I know I can't possibly justify that statement. I'd just like to raise the point though, that perhaps a purely CPU thing is not representative of installation throughput in a scientific job shop.

Dr. Wichmann: Yes, I accept those comments.

Mr. Curnow: Maybe the reason is that the scientists get a good big CPU and the commercial people concentrate on getting a good I/O, which they know about.

A Case Study of a Commercial Benchmarking Application–I

Maurice Blackman

Arthur Andersen & Company

I'd like to say a few words by way of introduction about Arthur Andersen & Company because, since we are basically a chartered accounting firm, there are probably a number of you here who haven't heard this before. The chartered accountancy arm is by far the largest component of the company, but we do have a management consultancy arm, and my role in the company is the computer consultancy part of the management consultancy division. Part of our professional services is the evaluation of computer proposals to help our clients to select equipment. It is just such a case that we are using for an illustration this afternoon. My role in this particular case was that I was the project manager and as such was responsible, to some extent, for setting the work program. Mr. Otway and I insisted that we use the technique of benchmarking, against Mr. Otway's better judgement to some extent, at the beginning of the exercise. He will, of course, talk about the details of a benchmarking test, and I don't really consider myself qualified to do that.

The part of the topic that I'm going to cover is the process of evaluation that we went through with this particular client to get to the point where the benchmarking exercise, as such, played a role. I think it's rather important that you understand the environment within which we were using benchmarking, so that you can appreciate the significance of the results and, to some extent, the scope of the benchmarking exercise. I would hate people to go away from this conference with the view that we were using it inappropriately. It was in a very limited situation, and we thought it was appropriate for that particular situation, but we don't necessarily claim that this is repeatable in every job.

I'd like to start by saying a few words about the general pattern of our equipment evaluation process. There is a series of stages that we go through; the first is the establishment of equipment parameters. By this we mean a study of the work that the client requires the system to do, and at least a first stab at deciding what sort of configuration is going to be appropriate to his particular work. At this point, we would go as far as to determine whether we should have one processor or two, whether we should be using discs or tapes for particular files in the system, the amount of slow peripheral capacity that we needed—a general statement based upon a study of the work that is to be done in the installation to determine the general configuration.

The second stage is to establish the specification book. This is first and foremost a description of the work that is to be done in the installation. Apart from that, its purpose is to describe and dictate to the manufacturers the format in which they should present their proposals. We not only require them to present certain chapters, for example on costs, machine timing, and the conversion work that has to be done, should this be required, but we also specify quite closely the methods that should be used in presenting the data in each of those chapters. So the specification book is, first of all, a description of the work to be done in the installation and then, secondly, a statement of how the proposals are to be made. This, as you will understand, makes it somewhat easier for us to compare the proposals one to the other. There is a danger in a more unstructured situation of not really having data that is comparable at all.

The next point I'd like to make is on the question of selection criteria. It is a rule of our practice that the decisions that are made at the end of our evaluation process are made by the client. This, as you know, is a standard defense for professional people; they only give advice, they do not make decisions. We do follow this quite closely and by that means, hopefully, avoid some of the problems when we come to collect our fee. The particular criteria that we identify for computer selection is classified into two groups. First of all, qualifying criteria, by which we mean certain aspects of the performance of the equipment that the manufacturer of that equipment must meet in order to be considered further. Perhaps a simple example of this might be the delivery date in a particular circumstance because the client requires to start a particular piece of work at a certain point in time and there is no purpose in proceeding with a manufacturer that cannot deliver his equipment at that point in time. The second group are what might be described as comparative criteria, which range in importance from extremely important, such as cost, to less important, but nonetheless of interest, such as experience in the same industry as the client. So we have two sections, then, of qualifying criteria and comparative criteria, and we establish these in consultation with the client partly by inviting him to say what his criteria are. If any of you have posed that sort of question to people, you will know that you don't get a very sensible answer. We also find out indirectly by means of discussions what appear to be the important characteristics of the total package; machinery cost, development simplicity, and so on. The end result is to present a statement of what we understand to be the criteria, classified between qualifying and comparative and then ranked between most important and least important. We also ensure that the client understands that this is the process that we are going to go through in evaluating the proposals. So the manufacturer's proposals and the evaluation of those proposals, together with the negotiation of certain doubtful points, like whether there's a discount allowable on disc drives, for example, proceed in parallel up to the point where a report is made to the client on which he can base his decision. It is the area of the evaluation of the proposals that we are concerned with this afternoon.

A few words about our client. In this particular instance he wishes to remain anonymous, but we can say that it was one of the regional boards in a utility industry in the U.K. The major reason for bringing this in at all is because there is a certain characteristic about his workload that was most relevant in this evaluation and in our decision to use benchmarking techniques. The relevant point was that the energy sales and billing application, although possibly commercially not too significant in terms of the profitability of it as an application, was nonetheless the lifeblood of the installation. It concerned a volume of data of the order of two million commercial records of approximately 500 characters each, a quite significant data base. This was too big to process every day and was therefore treated as other utility industries do in the U.K., on a quarterly basis. A day's run was on 1/60th of the billings for that particular quarter.

The other applications, which are all linked together to feed their eventual accounting and reporting application, did not contribute significantly to the overall computer load. They were either weekly or monthly runs, and they tended to work on much smaller files than the two million records on the customer master file. The reason for the job arising at all, incidentally, was that the application was in the process of conversion from a series of different applications installed by different parts of the Board, and the conversion had got to the point where something like a third of the accounts were on the main computer, and it was becoming quite evident that it was going to run out of capacity soon. There were certain other characteristics that the manufacturer exhibited that the Board was not too happy about, so they determined that they had to review not only the capacity of their equipment, but also the supplier as well. That really is where we entered the picture.

Among the selection criteria that we use in coming to an evaluation are the group that we described as qualifying, and in this particular instance, because of the tremendous significance of this billing application in terms of its use of resources, it was determined that one of the qualifying criteria was that the equipment had to be able to run the daily billing application in the time available on each day. It's absolutely crucial that each day's billings get done within a 24-hour time span because the following day's billings are right there waiting to be done, and if you lose a day then catching up again can be quite catastrophic. So it was a qualifying criterion, in this particular instance, that the equipment should have the capacity to run the daily billing system within a time limit of seven hours. This was arrived at by subtracting the amount of time it took for data preparation and the amount for report distribution from the total machine time available during the day. So there was a seven-hour time limit for a very specific system.

In evaluating the capacity of the equipment proposed, we weren't really seriously interested in any theoretical measurements of capacity. We were concerned instead with the actual system that the Board was running or would be able to run in the seven hour period. It was a fairly significant system in terms of lines of coding; there was no opportunity anyway, since it was coded in a low level language, to attempt to run the real system or the real programs of the real system on each manufacturer's equipment. What we did was to attempt to model the real system using simulations of each individual program, but the model as a whole represented the real system. Is that clear—the distinction between the system and the program? It was a representation of a real system, but the individual programs were in themselves modeled. I'll get on to the method of modeling in a moment. We were also in a rather fortunate position in doing this modeling work in the sense that the application did already exist, and it was running successfully on the equipment available. We were therefore able to verify that our model bore some relationship to the truth because we were able to test the model first of all against the existing equipment before attempting to use it to evaluate the new equipment being proposed.

We presented a complete statement of the system in terms of a systems flow chart to each manufacturer in the specification book. The individual programs within the system were therefore identifiable, and the files that each program accessed were identifiable. The system flow chart was supported by a description of the system with three or four line synopses of the purpose of each program so that the business function was quite clear. The file volume data were presented in tabular form and the files being identified were keyed back to the system flow chart. The medium of each file was stated, together with the number of records and their sizes. The hit rate, in respect to any files that were directly accessed, as well as the instructions to the manufacturer to tell him how he should go about the theoretical timing, were also included.

The manufacturer was required to calculate the processing time that each program was predicted to require. He was also required to calculate the input/output time and, therefore, be able to come to a statement of how long each program would run. The processing time was subdivided between application-dependent processing and software-dependent processing. The application-dependent processing was based on the model statement of the application programs. The software-dependent processing was the standard operating system functions connected with data movement. We have to face up to the problem, as I say, of how to represent the real system without using the real processing code. We worked on the basis of considerable experience within our firm—we have been working in the computer field since 1953, and we have done a fair number of installations and evaluations in that time. It's been our observation that the commercial programs are, in general, made up of large numbers of small modules that can be grouped into a small population of types. The individual examples of each type of module obviously differ in terms of which instructions they use but, by and large, it appears from our observation that the processing carried out in application programs can be classified. They can be classified between arithmetic modules, relatively simple arithmetic modules in commercial processing, editing modules, and general processing of the type that Mr. Berners-Lee referred to. The modeling that we did worked on the theory that we could represent the processing in an application program in the commercial area by describing each of the different processing paths within one program as comprising a number of different types of module (see Table 1). For example, the processing of a master file update to change a customer's name and address might consist of two A-type modules, no B-type modules, and one C-type module, and then the number of master file updates that we expect in a particular run can be used to extend that and give us a statement of how many modules are going to be generated by that particular piece of processing.

Let's have a look at one of these modules in some detail, and I think perhaps it will make somewhat clearer the extent to which we define them. If we draw a flow chart of the module, which we describe as type A, and assume that we'll use a high-level language (no specific high-level language, it's more precise English than anything else), the manufacturers are required to code this module and, in fact, the other two as well, in whichever language they are proposing to use in the system that we are timing. It seems that they have some work to do.

First of all, compile any individual module in order to develop a statement of which machine instructions are going to be used in each module and, therefore, how long each single module will take to run. The data fields that are referred to in the flow chart are then in themselves defined with reference to certain characteristics of the client's own processing. Again in this particular instance we were able to inspect the system; we were able to

TABLE 1   Modular examination of a commercial application program

		Modules		
Programs	Function	Type A	Type B	Type C
BM010	—	30,000	15,000	15,000
BM035	Additions	3,000	1,500	—
	Updates	180,000	120,000	—
	Mismatch	1,500	1,500	—
BM050	—	81,000	81,000	162,000
BM030	Master mismatch	36,000	18,000	—
	Match	180,000	120,000	—
	Trans. mismatch	6,000	3,000	—

inspect the record layout, and we were able to get a reasonable understanding of what sizes of fields, what types of data representation were used and, therefore, satisfy ourselves that these modules were going to be representative of this particular client's processing. I can't stress this too much; this is not presented as a general method of benchmarking using exactly these figures and exactly these flow charts, but more that it was representative of this particular client's dominant application. I do want to keep that before you all the time.

This statement of the processing path, then, within each program was established by inspection of the flow chart and the coding related to each program. The number of each program is stated so that this can be keyed to the flow chart and then the major processing functions of each program were listed, and by inspection of those processing paths we were able to come to an understanding of how many As, Bs, and Cs were required for each cycle. Then, by inspection of the volumes of throughput in terms of both transactions and master files, we were again able to state how many cycles we could expect to see executed in a representative run of the real system.

Obviously, we have to exercise some judgement here. We have to come to a professional opinion as to whether these numbers of As, Bs and Cs are going to be representative of the actual programs, and, in this particular instance, we were fortunate in having a running system so we were able to use this statement of the model of the real system, substitute the processing times appropriate for the particular processor in use, establish what the theoretical running times using this model should be, and then compare them with actual running times of the real system. Not just any old day's run, but carefully prepared mock-ups of transaction tapes that were able to isolate these various processing functions for us. This meant that, for example, we could put up a transaction tape with no transactions on it and pick out the processing cycles that were determined by the master file. Equally, we could put up a transaction tape that only had new records on it or only had receipts or only had orders. So we were able to take a number of different runs of varying characteristics and, if not prove that this was the right model, at least demonstrate that it corresponded with the truth.

The manufacturers in their proposal were required to present a theoretical statement of what their proposed equipment would do in terms of running this model system as compared with the time limits allowed. We asked them to compare the channel time as against the processing time and come to a run time for each program, to select the larger of those and therefore, by summing all the programs, come to a predicted statement of the running time for the entire system. Now this, as they say, is where the story really starts, and at this point we needed to use a benchmark run to verify that the manufacturers' predictions of the processing time of the system were accurate. Mr. Otway will continue the story from here.

A Case Study of a Commercial Benchmarking Application–II

Mark M. Otway

Arthur Andersen & Company

We have, then, two alternative methods. One was to attempt to model exactly the capacity test specified in the specification book; this would have two disadvantages. The first disadvantage was that there were in the U.K. at the time no configurations of exactly the same size and channel configuration as the manufacturers were proposing, and the other problem was that we would then have needed to have a benchmark that lasted seven hours, which didn't seem too reasonable. So we took another approach, which was to attempt to verify the parameters that had been specified to us by the manufacturers and also, in a sense, to attempt to verify the timing method that we had specified in the specification book. (As an aside, I would point out that we would tend to use the direct capacity test method for much smaller machines than the ones we were talking about.) Now we use software to do this. This software consists of a set of Cobol programs, actually Cobol shell programs, which come in two types. The first are file generation programs. They are used to generate files of specified record lengths, organizations, and volumes that you specify by means of file characteristics or parameters. The second kind of programs are also Cobol shells—we call them simulator programs. They contain at various points exits where you can put in the A, B, C modules that were specified earlier, actually coded in the language proposed by the manufacturer. There were four of these

123

simulator programs, which attempted to simulate a validation program, a sequential update of a tape master file, an indexed, sequential direct access update, and an edit and report formating program. So that was the sort of system that we were intending to use.

What we actually did, and I'd like to emphasize again that we were testing the parameters specified to us, the software times, the hardware times, the seek times, and the timing method, is we specified a small system, called a *model system*, which is different from the capacity test system. This consisted of one run of each of these simulated programs. So, having specified this model, we then needed to do the following things: The first thing that was needed was that the A, B, C routines and the Cobol programs were converted by each manufacturer to his own machine, which was not a very large job. It consisted mainly of changing the file handling and of coding up and punching up what they'd specified in the proposals. They then needed to specify to us the benchmark configurations that we were going to use, which didn't have to be exactly the same as those proposed. They needed to have the same CPU and they needed to have the same kind of peripherals, but the channel configurations and the numbers of peripherals did not have to be the same. We could then carry out a theoretical timing of the benchmarking configuration on precisely the same lines as the manufacturers had done in their proposals, and we were then able to run this model system using the simulated programs so that we could compare the actual times we got with the theoretical times.

It's probably useful to say here that one of the reasons we took the approach we did was that we had a limited time scale, and the amount of effort that we had to put in for the whole of this benchmark was about four to five man weeks with an unquantifiable amount of help from the manufacturers.

We wanted to use four simulator programs because we had index sequential accessing programs in the real system, so we had both updates, a validate, and an edit. We also wanted to time a sort. We more or less arbitrarily varied the device types for intermediate files; we wanted to have sorts that had tape in and disc out, that type of stuff. The volumes of this model system were very much reduced from the volumes of the real system. We wanted to come to a benchmark run time of about an hour, give or take a few minutes, which was a reasonable time scale. Again we used more or less arbitrarily varied record sizes; some of the files were fixed length, some of them were variable length. We also needed to specify to the software system the A, B, C analysis and the number of processing functions carried out by the update programs. The processing functions are specified by the structure of the simulated program—we don't have any opportunity to change that. There was the indexed sequential update program, the edit, and the validate. You can specify how many additions should be done for each set of master file records as a percentage parameter, and you can say that you know we're going to add 10 percent of this file, that sort of stuff. We had had three proposals; Honeywell in their full configuration was proposing a dual 60/40 with fast discs and tapes, IBM was proposing a 370/158 using OS/VS1, and ICL was proposing two 1904Ss under George 3, one 1904S to run the major billing system and another one as back-up.

We were therefore faced with fairly diverse architectures and philosophies to the solution of how to run this system. Now, in contrast, the actual benchmark configurations that we used were fairly obviously not exactly the same as the configurations proposed. We had a single 60/40 from Honeywell with two discs and three tapes, we had a 370/158 configuration available to us with fewer discs and fewer tapes, although the same size and the same type as specified in the proposed configuration. We had one weirdie which was that ICL was able to provide a fairly large benchmark configuration. However, in the time scale that we were talking about, and I say this happened in the space of four or five weeks, they were not able to get EDS 60s on this, so we actually ran the benchmark using EDS 30s which have very, very similar characteristics, apart from data density. ICL, in fact, offered to run a separate test to show that an EDS 60 met the parameters, but we did not need to use them because we were fairly satisfied with the benchmarks that we had carried out.

So what results did we get? At first sight (Table 1) Honeywell appeared quite a lot faster than everyone else, but I'd like to emphasize that there was a reason for that. I would like to emphasize that the purpose of the benchmark was to compare the theoretical run time on the model system with the actual run time measured on the model system, and not to compare the overall run time between manufacturers for this small model system. The reason for this was two-fold. In the Honeywell case we had a particular problem, and that was the place where we conducted the benchmark was some distance away and we hadn't much time left. We had a little bit of a problem, and we were not able to run the indexed sequential update program, which was by far and away the largest, in terms of time, and that's why they are apparently a lot faster than the other two. The IBM and ICL figures in Table 1 are very close to each other, but

TABLE 1   Comparison of different benchmark configurations

	Honeywell	IBM	ICL
CPU	6040	370/158	1904S
Storage	64K words	2 megabytes	192K words
Discs	2xDSU190B	2x3330	9xEDS30
		1 controller	1 controller
Tapes	3xMTH502	3x3420 model 5	8x2505
		2 controllers	2 controllers
Theoretical results (secs)	729	3700	3500
Actual results (secs)	738	4100	3700

in fact this is fortuitous because they had very different channel configurations and slightly different block sizes. This was because we had taken the position that we would not be too rigid on block sizes because of the fact that the different machine architectures had different disc layouts and that therefore we would be reasonably flexible on block sizes, within limits. The thing that was important was that we got an agreement, give or take about 10 percent, which, if we go back to what the objectives were, was that the parameters specified to us and the timing method we had used agreed. By that I mean the theoretical timing, based on those agreeing with an actual timing of a system run in precisely the same way as the model system, was specified within 10 percent, and therefore, by what I suppose you'd call an inductive process, we were able to say that that sort of variance would occur on the calculated timings for the full billing system. Therefore we were able to give a professional opinion on the ability of the configurations specified by the manufacturers to meet the original seven hour time limit and that, indeed, we did.

So, finally, what did we gain? What were the advantages of the method? Basically, as I have said before, we had a very limited time period; the method we used did not require a great deal of effort; we did not need a detailed knowledge of the architecture and exact software characteristics of each manufacturer's configuration. The results could be understood by the client in that we said, this is the theoretical run time of the benchmark system and here is the actual run time. This method could be used for a projected system because, although there was a system running and it did have the same processing functions, it actually had a different file accessing method from that proposed by two of the three manufacturers. One alternative to taking this approach, we say, was to run part of the actual system, which would have required a large conversion effort because the existing system was written in a low-level language. In fact, for efficiency considerations, the manufacturers were encouraged to specify low-level language so, consequently, there would have been a large development effort just to convert part of the system for the benchmark. The other alternative would have been some sort of physical measurements that would have required us to have detailed knowledge of hardware and software, which we did not have and which we could not get in the time available.

There are two other things that we did not cover. We had specified a theoretical capacity test for an on-line enquiry system, an enquiry system on the customer master file. We were not able to do any physical testing of that. Secondly there was a requirement, in the event of a hardware failure during the seven hours, to be able to run this on-line enquiry system and the batch system in the space of nine hours, and we had specified a simple iterative method of calculating the theoretical run time of that multi-programming situation. We were not able to test that, either.

In conclusion I'd like to stress that our objective was to pass a professional opinion on the ability of the proposed manufacturer's configurations to meet the seven hour time limit, and this benchmarking enabled us to have confidence in that opinion. It did not enable us to test capacity directly and was in no way an intellectually rigorous test. It was something that we did in the situation that we were in.

DISCUSSION

Roger Jeffereys (Burroughs Machines benchmarking team): The thing that worries me a little bit about what you have been saying is this very tight time constraint that you had on you, and I wondered if you would explain how this came about. As a member of a benchmarking team, I'd be a little worried that you were forced into the position where you had to assess a whole system, including theoretical study and production of a model, etc., in that time. Maybe I misunderstood what you said, but four weeks seems to me to be a very short time to do a big exercise like that.

Mr. Otway: I'm sorry. The complete evaluation was not four to five man weeks. Four to five man weeks was the amount of time that we, Arthur Andersen, spent on the setting up of the small benchmark that we carried out and the running of it. The actual running took us half a day for each manufacturer, but the specification of the model system was very quick. Most of the time was spent in dealing with the manufacturers who had taken the Cobol programs away and were converting them and checking that the conversion was realistic and the logic of the program remained the same. It was spread over longer than a four or five week period, but it took four or five man weeks of effort from us to set up the benchmark, not to do the whole evaluation.

Mr. Jeffereys: I think I understand you. So the manufacturers each had an elapsed time of somewhere around or just over four weeks in which to convert and make sure these programs worked. Is that right?

Mr. Otway: Let's go over the whole calendar. We started this work with the client in May of 1973. We issued the specification book to the manufacturers in August of '73, by which time we had defined the real system for the theoretical capacity test included in the specification book. The manufacturers had six weeks to prepare their proposals including their presentations of theoretical timings. We then took a further three months to evaluate the proposals including the running—preparation and running of the benchmark test. The time constraint, such as it was, was that the customer was in a particular situation where he wanted to convert his entire region to a single, unified billing system, and for this reason he wanted to do this as quickly as possible.

Frank Walker (Annan Impey & Morrish): Can you tell us what influence the results of the benchmark had on your overall final judgement as to which configuration to recommend to the client? Was it a very major part of the evaluation or, when you boiled it down, was it really of very marginal importance in the final choice? If you had not done it, would you have probably reached the same answer anyway?

Mr. Otway: The first important thing to remember is the distinction we made about qualifying criteria. It was absolutely crucial to the choice of any manufacturer that he should be able to meet this timing test. Any manufacturer that had been unable to prove to our satisfaction that he could meet this test was required to reconfigure until he could meet the test. That would obviously have a significant impact on the cost of the equipment. Supposing, to pick a name out of the air, IBM had proposed a 145, as in fact we suggested that they might do because the 158 was obviously tremendously powerful for the job in hand. It did, in fact, turn out that the 145 would have taken something like 7½ hours, and consequently it was extremely crucial that we did get the configuration right.

One other observation I might make is that the increments that we are dealing with in CPU power are very, very substantial, so it was not only important that this was tremendously accurate, but it was important that we did have the right size CPU because, since the power increments are tremendous, so are the cost increments, and that was where the significance came. In the event that each of the three manufacturers was able to propose configurations that met the time constraint, superficially it might appear that it wasn't too important, but it was absolutely crucial in determining that they had proposed a realistic configuration.

Since the period when we did this we've been carrying out an evaluation on a rather smaller scale configuration where again, to pick a name out of the air, IBM proposed in the first instance a System 3 Model 10, and when faced with a capacity test they were finally forced into the position of having to propose a 370/115. I'm not suggesting the manufacturers are rogues and vagabonds at all, but simply that the amount of effort that they can afford to spend on one particular proposal is obviously not unlimited.

Inaudible questions

Mr. Otway: The answer to your first question is: the reason that we had to do this was that it was our professional opinion, and we had to state with our hand on our hearts and our heads on the chopping block that these configurations, in our opinion, would do the work. In that sense it was not necessarily a check of, is what this manufacturer proposed too big or too small? It's more, can we say with confidence that that configuration will do the job? There were, in fact, a lot of other factors, in the second group of criteria, that were compared by manufacturers.

There is another aspect of this situation. You will recall that I mentioned that the existing equipment had run out of steam part of the way through conversion. That configuration was proposed after all the information was made available to the manufacturers. I wouldn't say that the manufacturers used that information to make their original proposal, which then ran out of steam. Nevertheless, if they had exercised their very professional judgement to a sufficient extent one would imagine that they would never have arrived in this situation. Because it was so important to the client, we took a professional stance, if you like, but we had to reassure him that this time he'd obtained enough equipment, and also that this time he had not obtained too much equipment, because that costs money as well.

Mr. Greggains (Unilever): A simple question, perhaps. It sounds as if you did this some reasonable period ago. Is the machine now installed, the unnamed machine at the unnamed client's premises, and is it performing as you predicted? It's one of the few chances to get a before-and-after study of a benchmark.

Mr. Otway: Unfortunately, the order was placed in January of this year, and the machine will not be delivered until the middle of next year, so we're not, as yet, able to verify that we were right. Well, we do have a continuing relationship with the client so we'll still be in trouble. We do, I think, have one caveat that we can put in there. We were dealing with three different manufacturers, three different sorts of architecture, and in no case did the manufacturers complain about the benchmark so we are reasonably confident that other professional people share our judgement that this is a valid test of their equipment's capacity. Until we can actually prove otherwise, we still feel reasonably confident.

Richard Jones (Harwell): Could you tell us if one of these proposed configurations was an upgrade, or were they all completely different from what your clients had inhouse already?

Mr. Otway: Yes, one of the three manufacturers was the incumbent.

Mr. Jones: It wasn't an upgrade then?

Mr. Otway: It wasn't an upgrade in the sense that it was a respecified configuration, no. They were upgrading parts of it to effect the conversion and bringing other things in, but it was really a completely respecified configuration. It wasn't just adding on bits to the existing configuration.

Mr. Jones: You said that this large application was in a low-level language. To what extent did conversion problems play a role in your decision-making?

Mr. Otway: Well, in the client's decision-making they had a very large role. Cost was one of the comparative factors, and the costs were broken down into quite a lot of things, such as a five year cash-flow period, and conversion. Indeed, we did a great deal of work in passing another professional opinion on the validity of the conversion efforts that had been specified in the proposals.

Mr. Jones: Can I make a guess that it is very likely that you would have stayed with the same manufacturer anyway!

Mr. Otway: I am sorry to be so mysterious about this business, but you will appreciate that client confidence is a rather important thing for us.

J. F. Dunnet (American Express IBC): I'm not sure whether I have actually got the gist of what you've been saying, but it seems to me that you developed a theoretical model and a theoretical manner of estimating the effect of these three types of new equipment on the user's workload, and then used a benchmark purely to gain confidence in that theoretical model. Was that the case?

Mr. Otway: Precisely. The basis for proving this confidence in using the technique at all is that the firm has used it over a considerable period of time. It is a standard approach in that we use a similar technique in most evaluations where capacity is a significant factor.

Mr. Dunnet: So this surely rings the death knell of benchmarking. Can we all have your theoretical methods please?

Mr. Otway: No, I think not. As I tried to explain, there is in this particular instance a particular reason for wishing to benchmark some of the key factors in the capacity test. In a lot of circumstances, where we would be dealing with small equipment, we might use only the benchmarking method and model the real system using the simulator that we have. In fact, several of our colleagues in offices on the continent have done exactly that, and they say to us, why do you go through all the trouble of hand-calculating this theoretical run time when all you need do is put it on the simulator and run it through? In this particular instance we wanted to be doubly sure, if you like, that this was a reasonable check of the capacity, so we did it both ways.

The simulator also would not have been a good simulation of the real billing system, where the major update program had a lot of files and was very large and had a lot of processing functions. The Cobol simulator system that we had just could not cope with something that big. So, fine, if you are testing something of System 3 or 2903 small machine size, we would tend to try and run realistic volumes through a system that is merely validate, update, edit. But in this situation the system was just too big to attempt to run realistic volumes through it, and the programs would not have been a realistic size.

Mr. Dunnet: Yes, I take that point, but surely that's a problem that a good many companies in the commercial field have. For instance, if we wanted to run a truly representative benchmark we would have to run a full month's work, which I don't think any manufacturer would like. This has been stated to be the main problem, trying to find out what to run as a benchmark. If one could work out some magical formula, or some manner of theoretically taking the workload and converting that into figures, and then applying that to information passed by the manufacturers, this would, in effect, do away with benchmarking, other than as a verification stage.

Mr. Otway: The problem is that we are only a very short way along that road. As we said in the talk, we were very lucky. We had a very dominant daily system which was run alone in the machine, barring some spooling, and therefore we had a fairly simple identifiable analytical case. We didn't have the problem of the payroll runs on Tuesday with the sales ledger and it's got to be out by 9 o'clock at night. If the configuration specified was able to run this very big system, it would eat the payroll and all the other accounting systems with no trouble, because it was so dominant.

Mr. Bayly (ICL): As I said this morning, I completely agree with this approach to benchmarking. I think since people may think it's the ultimate approach I'd better put some limitations on what I've said. The sort of thing that you can't do with this technique is, for instance, to predict the effects of certain features of modern architecture of machines that are, as it were, store-based. We, as manufacturers, have moved in improving the architecture of our machines from making it go faster and faster in its logic, to the actual way it fetches data from store. I don't mean the backing store, I mean the actual main store of the machine, and this method of emulation that we use quite extensively to represent background workloads, as we call them, cannot be used in this simple way for that sort of work. So, though I back the technique, I'm afraid it is limited.

Mr. Otway: Yes, our point was that we didn't actually care too much which was the most elegant solution, just that there was a solution.

Mr. Bayly: Yes. I wasn't being critical of your method, I was just making this comment in general.

A Case Study of a Multi-Access Scientific Benchmarking Application

R. S. Brown

Computer Systems Division,
Post Office Telecommunications

(What follows is not a verbatim transcript of what was said, but the paper the author issued describing what was going to be said. It is a close approximation to the lecture. *Editor*)

INTRODUCTION

A method of assessing the performance of a multi-access system is presented. It is based upon a series of tests derived to investigate the performance of a number of multi-access systems as part of the selection exercise of a new, large scale system to meet the scientific computing requirements of the Post Office Telecommunications Headquarters. This paper contains

1. A general description of the method, with comments, and
2. An examination of a case study that demonstrates the use of the technique when it was subsequently applied to study the effects of a revised operating system and the use of a communications front-end processor on an existing inhouse computer.

METHOD

Generation of Workload

Live or Simulated Users?

One of the first decisions to be made in the preparation of a multi-access test is whether it is to be a live test or with simulated users. The live test is conducted using a cross-section of users seated at the maximum required number of terminals, and the simulated test employs an external computer that executes the scripts at defined rates and communicates with the computer under tests representing normal terminal activity. There is much conjecture as to which method is the more representative and reliable, and each has its own advantages depending on the application. However, as a general guide, the live test is to be preferred for tests forming part of an evaluation-and-selection exercise and for special investigations such as the comparison of alternative operating systems, whereas the simulated test is more acceptable where the results are to be contractually binding, such as in the case of an acceptance test. The advantages and disadvantages of live and simulated tests can be summarized as follows.

Live test: These are more difficult to arrange in practice due to problems of finding and training large numbers of terminal operators. Also, it is vulnerable to human errors at the terminal, which can alter the workload, and in the worst case terminal misoperation can crash the system. A further problem with live tests is that if the test is repeated, as the terminal operators become more familiar with the scripts, then the time spent in thinking and typing falls. The effect of this is that the throughput appears to improve with successive runs of the same test. In the case study described here the total time spent in thinking and typing fell during three successive runs by a factor of 23 percent. However, the results obtained from a live test are always more convincing than those from a simulated test, and the live test does allow subjective assessment. The value of subjective assessment by participants with sufficient previous experience should not be underestimated. Probably the most significant advantage of the live test is that it does allow a wide range of responses and elapsed times to be easily measured by the terminal operators, thus eliminating the need for extra software to record the various measurements.

Simulated test: The obvious disadvantage of this method is the need to provide a second computer either onsite or via access over PO lines. This method is not susceptible to typing errors but is prone to getting into a regular pattern of activity not representative of the typical live load. Not the least of the difficulties is the need to select a *think time* which is defined as the time spent in thinking and typing in a command. Usually this is constant, and thus the second computer will wait the same period on every occasion before transmitting the next message. A system that provides for a distribution of think times about a mean would be much superior. The common error is to choose a time that is too short. Obviously, in reality this time varies from user to user and with the nature of the work, but in the author's experience with a number of live tests a think time of between 20 and 25 seconds is typical. Unfortunately, the value of think time has a very significant influence on the performance, and therefore should be given much consideration.

However, it is a fact that in the simulated test the think time is at least known and predictable, that this method is to be preferred for an acceptance test since this facilitates the establishing of acceptance performance tests.

Scripts

The multi-access performance must be assessed for a workload profile equivalent to the one that will be generated by your organization. In order to do this the current usage is examined by analyzing scripts produced by users at sample terminals, if available, and information logged by the present system about terminal use. The next step is to generate scripts that represent the predicted workload profile. Scripts should be created in such a way that no script contains programs written in more than one language. It is then possible to include the different scripts in the required proportions of the different languages to be used, such as Fortran, Algol, BASIC, PL/I, etc.

Within a script there should be three distinct phases: editing, compilation, and execution. It should be arranged that the scripts are commenced at different points by groups of users as this will prevent a build-up of users in the same phase.

Programs

In the execution phase, programs should be run that are similar in content to those that will be generated by your organization. In order to reduce the amount of coding, instead of writing separate programs to represent many varied applications it is preferable to write a small number of synthetic parameterized programs, which can be easily adjusted in terms of characteristics. These programs should contain a number of sections, each of which performs a particular type of work, i.e., interactive input/output to and from slow speed terminals, input/output to secondary storage, and, last, CPU-bound instructions. The sections should be contained within FOR or DO loops so that by setting the values of the limits that define the number of times each loop should be executed, the profile of the program can be adjusted at run time. During the execution of the synthetic program, elapsed and CPU times should be recorded programmatically at suitable intervals and printed out at the terminal.

A synthetic program widely used in PO tests was constructed in the following way. The program was divided into three sections: a terminal I/O loop, a disc I/O loop, and a processor-bound loop. The user was required to input parameters that specified the number of times each loop was executed. The contents of the loops were as follows:

Terminal Input/Output. Five numbers typed in by the terminal operator were typed back by the program.

Input/Output Disc Sort. Ten random numbers were generated, and each one was stored in the first element of a 100 word record of a disc file. Using the first element as a key, the records were sorted into ascending order.

CPU-Bound Loop. This loop represented a typical PO processor-bound program, synthetically produced by applying weightings to approximately 40 different types of statements.

Performance Criteria

No single result can be used satisfactorily as a single comparison factor. Benchmark tests generate an overall picture of each system, but it is always difficult and often a dangerous oversimplification to compare the performance of different machines using single isolated results. This is especially true in practice since it is rarely possible to create identical conditions on different systems, and therefore direct comparison is difficult; for example, in many cases different configurations will not be directly equivalent, or the number of terminals may vary. However, certain results are of greater value, especially when considered together, and are as follows:

1. *Response Time.* One of the most widely used parameters in measuring the performance of a multi-access system is the response time for commands. This is defined as the time between entering the last character of a command at a terminal and receiving the first character of the final processor output at completion of that task at the terminal. In assessing editing performance it is of great value to measure the response times for trivial tasks which require less than one processor time slice to complete. Although it is of interest to measure the response time for multi-time slice commands it is not particularly meaningful. The standard of response times to trivial commands should be defined by two quantities, namely:

    a.   Average time in seconds.
    b.   Percentage completed within a certain time.

In PO tests the commands that were classified as trivial were DELETE, INSERT, and LIST.

2. *CPU Allocation.* The CPU allocation is a measure of the proportion of CPU time given to a job and is normally expressed as a percentage. It is measured in the following ratio

$$\frac{\text{CPU time (Secs)}}{\text{Elapsed time (Secs)}}$$

It is of interest for CPU-bound work where it is a guide to the elapsed time that will be necessary to complete a job. In normal circumstances CPU allocation is a function of the demand for the CPU at the time. The standard of performance should be defined as the minimum, average, and maximum CPU allocations received by processor-bound jobs during the test. These should refer to the steady state period of the run, the period between the last user logging on and the first user logging off.

3. *Throughput.* This is assessed by looking at the overall time to complete the scripts, which includes the editing, compilation, and execution phases. The standard of performance should be represented as the average, shortest, and longest script durations of the different types of scripts in use.

Sources of Information

Data for the analysis of the run can be obtained from the following five sources:

CPU monitor

Central console log

System log

User console log

Scripts

CPU Monitor

It is often useful to have a means of monitoring the demand for the CPU throughout the run. A way of realizing this is to run a CPU-bound program at an equal priority level with the other scripts, from one of the terminals. The more this job is able to gain control of the CPU, the less is the total processing demand, and therefore in this way it is a measure as to how heavily loaded the system is at any point during the run. A software monitor widely used in PO tests executed a CPU-bound loop until a period of one minute elapsed time was exceeded, and then printed, at the terminal, the number of times the loop had been executed, normalized to one minute. It also printed the amount of CPU time used per minute. In normal circumstances the CPU monitor level will closely follow the CPU allocation being given to other jobs. The period during which the monitor receives its lowest allocation should coincide with the period when the lowest allocation is given to a user program.

Central Console Log

This plays an important part in the running of a test, as it shows how many terminals are logged in and to which lines, at any time. Also, in most cases it records the start and finish times for all compilations and executions. It also provides a record of which terminals logged off and when, towards the end of the run.

System Log

The system log records much useful information on each user's activities and often gives details of the usage of CPU time, I/O time, and memory for each program including editing routines. In a live test these results may be used to check the accuracy of response and elapsed timings made by the terminal operators, and whether the scripts were followed correctly.

Terminal Logs

The main information available from the user terminal printouts is the programmatically generated timechecks and CPU times. These are not always available when a simulator is used.

Scripts

Again, as with terminal logs, these are only available when the test is a live one. The scripts are a convenient place for the terminal operators to record the response time for each edit command. Also, the start and finish time of each of the phases should be recorded so that the durations of the phases and program elapsed times can be calculated.

CASE STUDY

Description of Tests

The following case study describes a series of three tests carried out by the PO on two similar inhouse computers. The tests were based on the technique described earlier in this chapter. The objectives were to compare the performance of the standard computer with the other, which is equipped with a front-end communications processor, and also to study the effect of the use of alternative time-sharing software.

The runs were as follows:

Run 1   11 January 1973
Standard operating system

Run 2   8 February 1973
Front-end processor
Alternative operating system

Run 3   20 February 1973
Front-end processor
Standard operating system

In each of the three runs, 15 live terminals were operated simultaneously, and the script distribution was as follows:

8 users performed an Algol script

4 users performed a Fortran script

1 user performed a BASIC script

1 user continuously ran a simulation program

1 terminal was used for running a CPU monitor program.

This reflected the relative use of the various compilers during a typical time-sharing session. Each Algol and Fortran script consisted of editing, compilation, and execution phases. The scripts were started at different points to prevent a buildup of users in the same phase.

Analysis

The most successful way to assess the performance of a multi-access system is to build up a picture using the various measurements available on a continuously varying basis for the duration of the run. In this way it is possible to determine at what stage in the run, for example, the slowest and fastest responses to a particular command occurred and to understand why. In other words, the behavior of the system throughout the run should be related to the load on the machine at the time. In addition, if circumstances allow, it is often useful to repeat the run with certain changes, such as the number of users, to see what effect this has on performance. In this way it is possible to identify the limiting resources.

For each run the number of terminals logged in at any time was plotted over the duration of the test. Also the current phase of each user was identified (editing, compiling, or executing) as shown in Figs. 1 and 2. All the terminals log in very closely to each other, but they log out over a much wider interval. Thus for a significant portion of each test, the number of terminals actually logged in is less than the maximum stated number. Also, for each run the distribution of response times to trivial commands was plotted in histogram form, as shown in Fig. 3. For each script the average response time to trivial commands was calculated. The periods during which the editing phase took place for the scripts with the shortest and longest average response times were identified on the dynamic graph of the run shown in Fig. 1.

Also for each run the minimum and maximum values of the CPU allocation ratio given to a particular job were identified on the dynamic graph of the run as shown in Fig. 2.

Finally, for each run the throughput was examined by drawing a histogram of the duration of each user's activities as shown in Fig. 4. On the dynamic graphs of each run the level of the CPU monitor was displayed using a suitable scale (in this case CPU seconds per minute), as shown in Figs. 1 and 2.

Results and Conclusions

Figures 1–4 refer to Run 3, and the following discussion also refers to this run and is presented to demonstrate the kind of

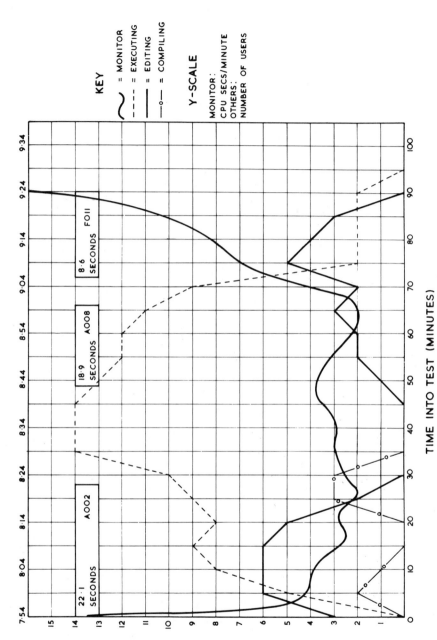

FIG. 1 How response times vary with machine times.

141

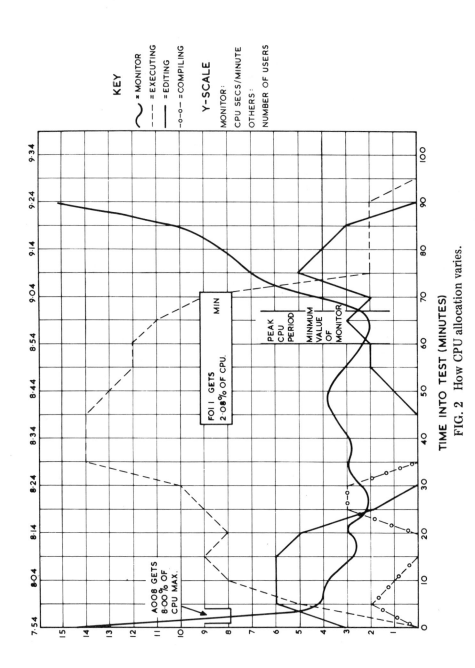

FIG. 2 How CPU allocation varies.

142

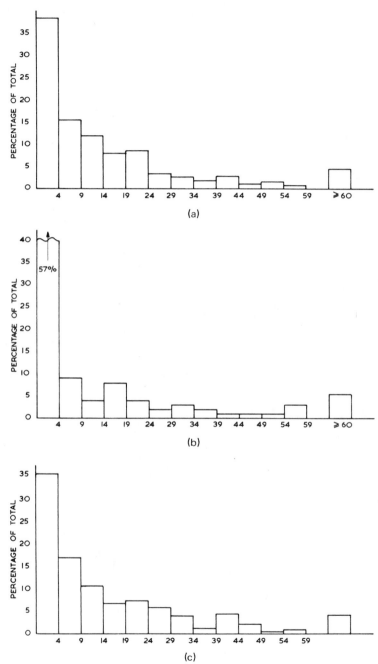

FIG. 3   Distributions of response times to trivial commands for
each run.

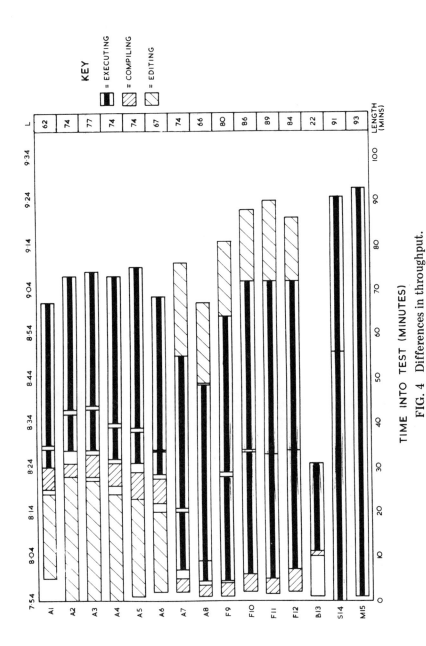

FIG. 4 Differences in throughput.

information that can be gained from a typical test. Figure 1 shows the average response to trivial commands at various stages of the run. It shows that the average response fell as the number of users declined (as is to be expected). Also, the degradation of response was greater when more users were editing than were executing. This shows that the limiting resource, during the periods when temporary overloads caused an increase in response time, was probably demand for I/O channels, rather than demand for the CPU. During the periods when the response times were worst the demands for the CPU was only moderate. The period during which the longest responses were recorded (average 22.1 seconds) was between 7:53 p.m. and 8:22 p.m., when there were up to nine jobs being executed and six being edited. The figure shows that later, despite an increased number of users executing programs, the response fell to an average of 18.9 seconds. This took place between 8:43 p.m. and 9:01 p.m., during which time there were between 11 and 13 users executing programs, but only 2 or 3 editing. The fastest response times were experienced between 9:06 p.m. and 9:24 p.m., when the average fell to 8.6 seconds. During this period there was both a reduced editing and reduced CPU load. The figure shows that the monitor occupancy was rising steeply during this period, indicating a diminishing CPU load.

Figure 2 shows how the value of the CPU allocation ratio depends on the load on the machine at the time. The highest allocation received occurred during an Algol compilation, where the value was 8 percent. This occurred between 7:55 p.m. and 7:58 p.m., at the very beginning of the test, before all the users had begun their scripts. Monitor allocation was falling rapidly but throughout this period was at a high level, indicating a low demand for CPU time. Monitor allocation was at its lowest value between 8:55 p.m. and 9:02 p.m., when it was receiving only 3.3 percent of the CPU time. The lowest CPU allocation was 2.08 percent, which occurred on a Fortran CPU-bound program between 8:37 p.m. and 9:05 p.m., when it received only 35 seconds CPU in 28 minutes. During this period there are between 14 users (at 8:37 p.m.) and 9 users (at 9:05 p.m.), all executing programs and thus presenting a heavy demand for CPU time.

By studying the results of all three runs in the same way the following conclusions were reached:

1. The addition of the FEP had a negligible effect on editing performance and throughput.

2. The alternative time-sharing software significantly improved editing performance, throughput, and CPU utilization.

Summary

The technique described represents a highly successful method of developing a comprehensive picture of the behavior of a system and of evaluating its performance.

DISCUSSION

Mr. T. Knowles (GEC Computers): Although you demonstrated that by using your benchmark load you have increased the speed of running of your benchmarks, have you any way of telling whether, in fact, you have increased your real live throughput? Has there been an increase in the rate of processing of useful work by the people using your installation to give a feedback on the validity of your benchmark?

Mr. Brown: Yes. The addition of the front-end processor has shown that in practice the editing performance has been improved, but we had no opportunity to test the improved software.

Mr. C. J. Pavelin (Atlas Laboratory): I am still worried about your CPU monitor. Surely if it is running at equal priority, it could drastically affect the benchmark, which you have gone to great pains to make representative, unless you typically run with a terminal job which is processor-bound.

Mr. Brown: The CPU load is part and parcel of the representative load. I agree with you—running it at an equal priority level has advantages and disadvantages. We have tried both and have found more useful information by running it at an equal priority level than by running it at a low level.

Dr. Buttle (Exeter University): What is the machine operating system that we are talking about?

Mr. Brown: Similar to the last authors, I am not able to divulge it for security reasons. I am not sure that identification of the machine is necessary to understand the points I have put forward. I know that the manufacturers are represented here, and I am sure that they would immediately identify the system.

Dr. Buttle: Perhaps that's true, but I am interested in the more practical aspect, apart from benchmarking, of how typical these response times are of other users' experience in multi-access environments. Approximately one-third of trivial commands get responses in less than four seconds. That means two-thirds have got to wait four seconds or more. What I am interested to know, although it is off the subject of benchmarking, is: is this typical of other users' experience with all sorts of machines?

Mr. Brown: Yes, it is typical with these machines, and we think it is a poor response time.

Mr. W. F. Wood (ICL): Figure 4 shows that there is a tendency for jobs to be in the same state at the same time. This seems a bit artificial or unrealistic. How exact is this "time into test" which, I take it, means the time the test has actually been running, and so it shows what state the job is in at that time? Why have you chosen to run things so that jobs tend to be in the same state at the same time?

Mr. Brown: That is valuable criticism. I did say at the outset that we did have staggered starts. Obviously, we did not go far enough in staggering the tests. Only by doing a multiplicity of tests could one eventually arrive at an optimum and, of course, that approach would be very expensive.

Mr. R. Jeffereys (Burroughs Machines): Did you consider a mixture of simulated terminals and live terminals? You did mention this as a possibility at the beginning of your talk. It seems to us (and we have done it, not in the U.K., but in the United States) that it gives a much clearer picture of what goes on when you simulate many terminals. Then you have a few terminals that you could use either to follow a script or to interrogate various properties of the system as you go along. I am particularly thinking of the first thing where you get one of these live terminals to follow a script and then you get the impressions that you wanted to from those few terminals that are actually live, while the rest of the system is being driven loaded by the simulated terminals.

Mr. Brown: It would have been a different test—it would not have been practical to arrange a simulator of any sort.

Mr. Jeffereys: The sort of thing I am thinking of are benchmarkings that have been done on a B7700 where there were several hundred terminals logged in artificially and there may be five or six logged in in real life. We have done smaller simulations on the 6700 in Rodwell House in London, where we have had 90 or so terminals being simulated and two or three running with people sitting at them.

Mr. Brown: Yes, I think this is a method to be commended.

Mr. R. Prendergast (Univac): Can I ask how many manufacturers you asked to do the original benchmarking exercise?

Mr. Brown: I am not going to answer that!

Mr. Prendergast: Let us say four or five—one is £100,000, so you expected the manufacturers to spend £500,000 on doing this exercise—is that right? And this is not an unusual situation.

Mr. Brown: This is the present situation—things are going to change. I think it would be a very wise move for customers to pay for their own benchmarks so that they would be more selective in the manufacturers whom they invited. I would not want this to be interpreted as a criticism of my own organization—I'm talking in general terms.

Mr. Prendergast: I think it is very bad to expect the manufacturers to spend that much money. I think you should have decided who you wanted, who was the most likely contender.

Mr. Brown: Yes.

General Forum

Mr. R. Jeffereys (Burroughs Machines): I am in the difficult position of wanting to address Mr. Hatt, although I think he has left the conference. One of the things he said was that the construction of machines should be separated from the writing of the software for them. It seems to me, certainly from the Burroughs point of view, that that is the worst possible thing you can do if you want a good running system. Part of the philosophy of designing Burroughs systems is that the hardware engineer and the software engineer, who are treated very equally at Burroughs, sit in the same office and talk to each other. If the software engineer sees that a particular problem is difficult to solve by software, he has a talk with the hardware engineer to see if he can solve it. This is why some of the strange operators exist in Burroughs' hardware; they are solutions to difficult software problems. Mr. Hatt was wanting to exclude this. The worst case is where you almost get it right and then the software man has to try very hard to get it really right. That is worse than not getting it right at all and having to do the best you can. Any comments?

Mr. Curnow (CCA): Those of us who have looked at Burroughs' machines must admire the overall concepts in putting hardware and software together in a unified manner. However, it does have some difficulties. For instance, if you have your own private language, shall we say, and it does not happen to be very closely akin to Algol 60, and you have a standard bootstrapping means of putting it onto almost any computer, you will find that you have difficulties when trying to put it onto the Burroughs 5500. The B6700 is a bit more flexible but, nevertheless, you can have difficulties. These difficulties can be almost insurmountable; for instance, on the B5500, a one-dimensional array is restricted to 1,023 elements. If you want a big expanse of core to arrange your own allocation of store, you have to put the whole thing into a two-dimensional array, and you pay a penalty in that respect. I think there is a rather delicate balance that one has to devise between making an architecture that is excellent for one particular language and a machine, say a 360, on which you can do a reasonable job in almost all languages, but that is devoid of any architectural structure, in the language sense at least.

Unidentified speaker: I agree. There are a lot of problems with building too many clever tricks into the hardware. It is perhaps easier to do it in special systems where you have hardware really dedicated to a specific job, and you are writing the whole thing, operating systems and applications software, for a one-off job.

Mr. Jeffereys: It may be a better way in some designs, where you do not even choose your op-codes but just have a lot of microoperators at your disposal, and you build software in between.

Unidentified speaker: Yes, that is rather a fascinating approach, but it also has its difficulties. One is that it is rather difficult to maintain security in a microprogram situation where you are handling several languages. The advantage of microprogramming is that you can really go to town on, say, Algol 60 or Cobol or Fortran or whatever it is on your machine, by putting in a lot of microcode with interpreted instructions that are suitable for those languages. What you really need, if you are going to run those in parallel, is some overall method of maintaining integrity and consistency, and that is pretty hard when you have got microcode, which is very undisciplined at the lowest level.

Forum Chairman I. F. Croall (The Atomic Energy Research Establishment): I think one thing has become increasingly clear. We started off yesterday with an orgy of destruction—everyone was saying that we should not do it, it was a waste of time, and so on. We have seen some practical examples of using what is a tool, one of a number of tools that we have to help us in assessment or choosing new systems. It is important to see it in that light. If nothing else has come out of the conference, I think it is important that those people who swore by benchmarking as being the be-all and end-all of this game will go away realizing that it isn't, and perhaps those of us who were totally cynical will realize that some people knowing and realizing those limitations have managed to make it into a useful tool.

Unidentified speaker (IBM): I would like to raise the question of the realistic operational considerations. If we take a benchmark as it is normally done, we eliminate delays like disc-mount and tape-mount delays, the operators going to lunch, etc., in order to get a repeatable type of job stream. If the delay is zero, it is certainly not variable. However, in measurements of large, real-life systems, like batch systems, I find that extremely substantial amounts of time are wasted in one way or another. On many large machines this is a more important constraint, despite very high levels of multiprogramming, than the CPU or the power of the discs or the power of the tapes.

Unidentified speaker: If you introduce such things into a benchmark, you have other interesting effects, for example, a higher degree of multiprogramming becomes more productive because the bottom priority stream now begins to operate in the gaps that exist in the high priority streams. So it is very important to do that to get a feeling in practice of how many streams you ought to be running. The obvious consequence is that if you ignore it and try to predict an absolute time, you are obviously going to be out by a large percentage. I think that you can use a benchmark to say that this machine is x times faster than that one, but not so easily (without taking account of operational delays) to say that this machine will do this work in seven hours, because nobody will operate it so perfectly. So I would really like to ask anyone if they have done benchmarks that take this into account and, particularly, benchmarks comparing one piece of software that has aids for operators, such as ensuring that the tapes are mounted before the jobs begin, with pieces of software that do not have such aids.

Mr. Croall: I would like to add something else in the same line, and that is, what happens when something goes wrong in the system? You are not measuring anything about the recovery of the system when it goes wrong.

Mr. R. Jones (Harwell): I think that IBM appears to be moving in the right direction with the way that they have apparently cut out some of the allocation bottlenecks. But you cannot risk building this sort of thing into a benchmark just because the operator's cycle time is so much slower than the rest of the system. Our friend from Univac was saying about the Oxford Benchmark that you can make it go n times faster merely by putting a faster line-printer on. Clearly, that is a ridiculous way to run a benchmark. You can make calculations as to what you are losing by this sort of thing, but I do not think you can risk making the whole system hang up because the operator has gone to sleep.

Unidentified speaker: There is a hardware solution, of course—to put all your tapes onto discs or photodigital storage, for example.

Unidentified speaker: Yes, there is a hardware solution, but the rest of us are faced with having to mount tapes and mount discs, and with the sort of delays where you say, "I will not start this job now because I am waiting for the input and I do not want anything else to interfere with it." I do know of one case of tests being done where simulated delays, allegedly measured in the installation, were fed into the benchmark and, in one case, we had a big piece of software that did a lot of things to help operators but, because of its storage occupancy, it caused one less stream of jobs to be run. In the other case, we had a fairly conventional piece of software that ran one more stream of jobs but, in this test, performed more slowly. That is the sort of result that I am interested in.

Unidentified speaker: A point I would like to make on this is that the purpose of benchmarking as I understand it is to try to evaluate one of the many components of a computer room operation, and one is trying to select or evaluate equipment or systems, excluding the number of variables that are controlled in other ways. I would have thought that the efficiency of operators is something you would have assessed once the chosen machine and system were in and running, and that you would cure any of the types of operating faults you were discussing by better training of the operating staff. In a sense it is a benchmark, if you like to evaluate the real running of the system once it is installed, but it would seem to me that to include that sort of pause in the evaluation of the system, while you are choosing the equipment, is to admit that there is no way of controlling operating staff, whereas, quite obviously, there is.

Unidentified speaker: When you have got the thing installed it is too late to make a major decision to use an entirely different piece of software and, surely, one of the major things of a benchmark is to evaluate software so that in the limit it may be found if it does not work at all.

Unidentified speaker: The whole strategy of the installation depends on making this choice before you order the equipment. When you do a benchmark with a piece of software, that is, say, 400kB, and solely designed to help operators, you suffer a terrific penalty with absolutely no benefits to offset it if you do not have these operating delays.

Unidentified speaker: Well, my people think that the use of software to solve that particular problem would have been a misuse of software. There are other ways of dealing with poor operating performance than trying to provide software that will enable you, if you like, to utilize the effects of poor operating performance.

Unidentified speaker: It would appear to me that you are in the area of scientific management and performance measurement of people, rather than in evaluation of equipment. Therefore, perhaps you should take it into account when setting your criteria for your benchmark, but not put it into your benchmark?

Previous speaker: Well, as with time-sharing systems, I am interested in the behavior of the system as a whole.

Unidentified speaker: In time-sharing systems you do not have control over the people using the equipment because they are independent people who are personally responsible for their own efficiency. But in a batch-processing system, considering the performance of operators in the computer room, they are under the control of the operations manager. There are various tools—I mean standards and procedures—like improved training, or improved methods of assembling of input for your production runs. These are independent of the quality and speed of the equipment and software.

Previous speaker: I am sorry, the system hangs together as a whole. If people are part of the system and the system is not human-engineered properly—that is what I really mean by time-sharing—if the human-engineering is wrong, it is the human-engineering you should correct and not by a system that will satisfy so-called "human-engineering."

Unidentified speaker: I think we are back to trying to recognize just where this tool called *benchmarking* fits in.

Unidentified speaker (Univac): I am changing the subject somewhat. I think that, possibly, in some ways, we have not really achieved what we should have achieved. I sympathize with the man from Unilever. I am not sure that he is here now, but we have not covered the commercial area. I do not really know how the commercial man sees the best way to solve the evaluation problems, whether or not it is benchmarks, because we certainly have not had much in the way of contributions. I find that our experience within Univac is that most large benchmarks do not come from the commercial user, they come from the Establishment. I am just wondering what the commercial users' view of benchmarking is, whether they see it as a valid tool, or if they would rather see benchmarking go another way? We have not really discussed their problems, such as large application packages that are available. Our conversation has been biased very much towards the absolute measurement of machine power.

Unidentfied speaker (Harwell): I can see that this is another area for us to fight. I am unconvinced about all this mythology about differences between so-called scientific and commercial computing. The only major difference seems to be that commercial people insist on using Cobol, which, for one reason or another, we do not particularly like. Our own machine at Harwell runs payrolls, etc., mixed in with scientific, real-time, multi-access, the whole gamut of work. When you look at the nature of the program they actually run in the computer, you find that there is not all that much difference between them. We have large data-base systems in the scientific world, in fact, probably larger data bases than many people use in the business world. One has to be very careful about drawing this mythical war between commercial computing and scientific computing.

Unidentified speaker: I would like to support the comments of the gentleman from IBM. It is part of a total system, and you have to take into account the archiving time, back-up time, system recreation, fetching the machine tapes out of storage—all these things count. I cannot really envisage how such things can be benchmarked as a whole except by, as someone suggested, putting a month's work through the machine, but there is still room for benchmarking. We do it when we change releases of software or when we enhance the system in, perhaps, fairly trivial ways. We find it a useful pointer in system-tuning and to ensure that we are going in the right direction. Coming to the real-time terminal stuff, the speaker from the Post Office mentioned it, just now. You can measure response times and throughput times of jobs, and all of this is still relevant, but it becomes difficult because these other subjective features are going to come in. We all know that the faster the turn-around time, the less time people spend thinking about what has gone wrong. Part of what you want to measure is really how good the diagnostics are, how many runs are taken on development—development is certainly a very large proportion of our computer time. I do not know how this can be measured but it is very much a part of the system, and I cannot help thinking that one is going to have to benchmark various aspects of the system and then put the whole lot together with different weightings for these different features. Any comments? It is not a unified thing, in my opinion.

Mr. Croall: Everyone is going to agree with you and probably offer you some more ideas that will make you more depressed.

Mr. Curnow: Almost eighteen months ago, we put through several test programs written in Algol 60. These programs were simple—say half a dozen lines each. We have a report explaining these results. The programs all contained common programming errors chosen because they are the sort of things that we know frequently appear in our real programs. Of course, the real programs are longer than these test programs. We ran these ourselves on one of their time-sharing systems. It was rather tedious work, but you can just give them to a junior programmer and let him get on with it, and they can find out how to use the system at the same time. Anyway, the results were uniformly disappointing. There was not anything to choose between the manufacturers except that they were all bad. There were about 25–30 tests, and the important point was that in five or six tests the results were so bad that it would have been impossible for an ordinary high-level language programmer to have made any sense of the diagnostics that were produced. I was staggered with these results, especially since the technology in trapping these errors is well known and has been published.

Unidentified speaker: I think the direction that the discussion has taken is a very profitable one and is in the area that is going to be of the greatest interest in the future. We do not know how to solve this problem of the measurement of facilities. It is not just a question of a catalogue of facilities—it is this question, like the diagnostics just mentioned, whether the job command language is a usable thing or not. How many commands you have to give, whether the syntax of the command language makes it easy for the kind of people who have to use it who may not all be Ph.D.s but actually use it in practice. Clearly, the assessment of systems in these terms may be much more important in the long run than the assessment of pure hardware performance. The way the LSI technology is going, the cost of providing CPU performance is taking a nosedive and is going to go on nosediving, so it is these other considerations, like the nature of the interface between the system and the human beings who have to use it, that are the ones that are going to become more and more important.

Unidentified speaker: I would like to ask Mr. Prendergast, as a manufacturer, to attempt to break down some of the difficulties. First of all, we have heard £100,000 mentioned as the cost of a benchmark. Where are the breakdowns of this sort of cost? Is it machine time and tuning up the system? If it is, you ought to be going back to your simulation models and doing the benchmark on the machine when you have the right configuration. Or is it other things? If we identify the problems in manageability and in cost, then we can attack the problems that are easiest to overcome.

Mr. Prendergast: The cost is very difficult to break down. Some of the costs I quoted excluded machine time and manpower. It varies with the benchmarks what percentage of work you do; there tends to be a very high conversion content. That is the physical conversion of tapes, and the conversion of programs is another problem. You can convert most of the programs quite quickly but the main thing is that you are doing it against time and probably not doing it in the best manner.

I might have given the impression that I was against benchmarks. I am not against benchmarks. I am against a lot of benchmarks that are run solely on the grounds that we have just discussed because they are purely speed measurements. They do not take into account the efficiency of compilers. Mr. Berners-Lee said that some compilers can get you to a running program in far fewer shots than other compilers. Some systems are a lot easier to use—for some systems you need people to write the control language, just to get your program into the machines. With other machines a trained monkey can do it. Benchmarks never measure this sort of thing. Again, it can be the skill of your particular people who are doing the conversion that enables you to get a job done quite quickly, but it may not be representative of what your machine can do in the real situation. We tend to put very good people on benchmarks, but in a real situation most users do not have all very good people and so, possibly, what we can do is not what the users can do. The users may want systems that look clumsy to people who are used to the system. But the users who do not have a lot of expert people want these clumsy systems because they are easier to use.

Unidentified speaker: I think that quite a lot of the problems manufacturers have with benchmarks result from objectives which are arbitrary. If there was a real need for a benchmark, I am sure a manufacturer would undertake it but if the objectives seem to be ill-formed they are much less enthusiastic because they do not know what they are trying to achieve.

Unidentified speaker: We have had experience in this conference of people talking about the difficulty of getting representative workloads, being aware of possible errors creeping in when writing benchmarks, being able to understand what is going on and to interpret the results. In our particular exercise the last question (What are we aiming for? Will 2 hours do it, 2½ hours, will 3 hours do it?) we have said we expect our workload to be processed in something like 2–3 hours. The claim that a tape must be got through in a certain time to pass the benchmark test, as we have discussed in this conference, does not make sense. So, on the one hand you have your idealists who want the user to be aware of the present state of the art and on the other hand you have your practical men who want to be 10 minutes better than somebody else.

Mr. Brown: I was not aware that it had been said that benchmarking was the whole answer, and at the beginning of my paper I made the point that our benchmarking formed only a part of the total exercise. Carried out in parallel with our benchmarking tests was a whole series of other investigations which covered, obviously, a comparison of the ease of use and the power of facilities provided by the job-command languages on all the different systems, which is obviously entirely separate from benchmarking. Also, we were able to input a whole series of programs to each of the different compilers with known language errors and to see which compilers identified which errors and how useful the diagnostics were. Lastly, we had another separate hardware evaluation of the system in terms of the technology used and its reliability.

I think it is important to recognize that benchmarking is only one means to an end. I, personally, see benchmarking as part of performance measurement. There are three techniques known to me: hardware measuring, software monitoring, and an empirical approach which is benchmarking, but this is entirely separate from the investigation and the assessment of all the other aspects involved in the selection of a new computer.

Unidentified speaker: How much money is spent on other aspects compared with benchmarking? If it is £100,000 on benchmarking alone, we know where the emphasis is. You can forget the rest.

Mr. Brown: Yes, I think it is true to say that the cost of all these other investigations is largely borne by the purchaser. We can justify the expenditure of £x if it saves the purchase of several million pounds of hardware that is not suitable in some way.

Unidentified speaker: Here are the things that I am going to assess before I buy this machine, and here they are in a ranking table.

Where would benchmarking come, and how much money would the others get? Benchmarking is costly for the person who originates it.

Mr. Brown: That is true, and, therefore, one would have to put much more emphasis on the results of the benchmarks than on the others. Benchmarking is going to cost you more.

Mr. Blackman: It might be of assistance to you to have a few more statistics on the Arthur Andersen Case Study. I mentioned that the evaluation process which we went through lasted for three months. Since this was not a conference on computer selection, I did not spend very much time considering what the other criteria were. We had three people working fulltime on the evaluation of the amount of effort we expended on the benchmarking, as Mr. Otway indicated, something like five man weeks out of 36 or 38. We spent a tremendous amount of time in assessing the capabilities of the software that the manufacturers were proposing, but we did it by a totally different technique from benchmarking. Included in specification book, as any of the manufacturers who answered would testify, there were about 200 specific questions about different areas of the software, subdivided between the operating software and the development software. This asked how the manufacturers solved particular problems in each of those areas, and then each area was subdivided again as in the operating software between the job-accounting system, the input/output system, the job-scheduling, and so forth. We had a questionnaire that extended over 30–40 pages of this specification book, and we evaluated the software on the basis of the answers to the questionnaire, setting out which features were omitted from which software manufacturer, which features were included, and giving a subjective assessment as feature by feature—which were better and which were worse. Benchmarking is not the only tool in computer evaluation, and for certain criteria in the evaluation, other techniques are more appropriate.

Mr. Kiviat: If I had to write down the sense of this meeting to most of the participants, I have it here in 11 letters—frustration. I think you will all agree with me. We started by hearing the manufacturers say that benchmarking as it is presently conducted is not worth the cost, which was not unexpected. Then Mr. Berners-Lee made a very profound observation about the sensitivity of the lapsed times to detailed workload structure. That is certainly a testable hypothesis of enormous significance to people who use analytic models or to people who want to use synthetic benchmarks. As a testable hypothesis, I think it is something that should be tested. It is hard to convince anybody that a synthetic benchmark is appropriate. A manager finds it difficult to relate to his workload; he does not understand that relationship, and he therefore demands more realistic proof. We need some theory, which we do not have, or at least some kind of structured approach to measuring and comparing workloads. As long as we cannot respond to questions such as we have heard today, "How does the NPL workload compare with my Cobol jobs?" in some quantitative manner, we will never progress collectively, we will just solve one's individual problems one by one.

The importance of benchmarks based on historical data, which most of us get involved in, must be placed in some perspective. We have heard that new capabilities modify user habits, and therefore the value of the historical benchmark is questionable when you are buying a truly new system. This means that we have to construct a benchmark mix where we have capabilities of the system that might be used. We do not even know if the manufacturer who wins will have the capabilities that we might wind up using, which poses a game of some kind. We have to be aware that the percentage of user code executed in the CPU is decreasing relative to the other code that is there—the applications, packages, data management systems, the operating system itself. We have to construct benchmarks that will test these things. The relationship between historical performance data and present computer system performance is not the same as it was several years ago. This is related to methods of workload profiling and relating workload profile of historical data to an expected workload profile.

I believe that we would all like to have heard more talks like the one from the Arthur Andersen people about organizations, benchmarking practices, and their procedures for selecting workloads and dealing with the manufacturer. I think we would all like to have seen more data on before-and-after benchmarking situations. We have seen no data, which is possibly only a consequence of the long time it takes to buy something and get it installed in the short time we have been interested in benchmarks. Nevertheless, now we need a theorist, not an empiricist, because we have no theories and little data.

We have seen the value of a conjunctive approach to benchmarking and simulation modeling and other forms of measurement; that is, they are not exclusive, they are things that should be used together. We have seen different uses of benchmarking that tend to confuse us unless the use is explained very carefully. Witness the question and the comment on the possible interference of the CPU monitor. Now let me tell you what I think the three uses of benchmarking are, and how they have quite different purposes. Its use as a function of demonstration is a kind of a go-nowhere situation. Does it work or does it not? When used for analysis, you are primarily interested in the direction of change of something. You are not interested in predicting or estimating absolute values. When used as a selection device, you are trying to predict absolute values. In the first case, benchmarking is really the only thing. In the second case, a model or a benchmark coupled with some statistical regression approach may be adequate. In the third case, models, not necessarily coupled with benchmarks, either as validation tools or some kind of supporting tool are necessary. We ought to state clearly what our interest in the benchmark is. We tend to get confused.

The comment about benchmarks not considering operational restraints is another illustration of the same phenomenon. We do not consider the different aspects of selection of benchmarks. One is the legal aspect of having a clear selection device that requires something that takes out the variability. The other is the need for prediction and the proof of adequacy, which our management requires. These two things somehow fight each other and, having one procedure, as some of you think we should have, that satisfies both issues, I do not believe is possible. A good evaluation procedure has been commented on as being beyond the scope of benchmarking—a list of criteria, each of which has some number of points, each evaluated independently, with a benchmark score as just one mark on the list. I think that is a procedure that all the people who do benchmarking will follow. It was wise to point out that this was not a symposium on computer selection but on benchmarking as a technique.

I have tried to summarize what I think have been the highlights and some of the needs that we have. I am not a pessimist with respect to benchmarking; I think it is necessary, and I think it is going to be with us for a long time. I think if we are to make progress we have to take out the little aspect of benchmarking that we are interested in and try and improve it, rather than try to pick nits with people who are using benchmarks for something quite different.

Appendix A: Schedule of Speakers and Participants in Benchmarking '74

Thursday, 19th September and Friday, 20th September 1974
Churchill College, Cambridge

THURSDAY, 19 SEPTEMBER 1974

Chairmen

Barrington, R. L., The British Computer Society
Laver, F. J. M., Former Board Member for Data Processing, The Post Office Corporation

Speakers

Berners-Lee, C. M., ICL
Hatt, Peter, Software Sciences Limited
Jones, Richard, Atomic Energy Research Establishment
Kiviat, Philip J., Federal Computer Performance Evaluation and Simulation Center, Washington, D.C.
Prendergast, Robert, Sperry Univac

FRIDAY, 20 SEPTEMBER 1974

Chairmen

Croall, I. F., The Atomic Energy Research Establishment
Kiviat, Phillip J., Federal Computer Performance Evaluation and Simulation Center
Wickens, Roy, Central Computer Agency

Speakers

Bayly, R. G., ICL
Blackman, Maurice, Arthur Andersen & Co.
Brown, Robert S., Post Office Telecommunications Headquarters
Curnow, H. J., The Central Computer Agency
Otway, M. M., Arthur Andersen & Co.
Sutcliffe, Dr. S. E., ICL
Wichmann, Dr. B. A., The National Physical Laboratory

PARTICIPANTS

Aldridge, K., North Thames Gas
Arnold, J., Ministry of Defence
Ashill, M. C., The British Computer Society
Askew, M. J., ICL Ltd.
Atkins, R., Price's Chemicals Ltd.
Bacon, J., Honeywell Information Systems Ltd.
Bamber, K., Unilever Ltd.
Barford, A. T., Nottingham Computer Services Ltd.
Benwell, N. J., Cranfield Institute of Technology
Blake, N. B., Rank Xerox Ltd.
Blom, M., National Nederlanden NV
Bowers, K. A., Central Electricity Generating Board
Butcher, L. F., Midland Bank Ltd.
Butcher, M. T., Norwich Union Insurance Group
Buttle, Dr., Exeter University
Carpenter, F., Computer Aided Design Centre
Chomet, S., Transcripta Books
Clark, R. R., South of Scotland Electricity Board
Clary, B., Digital Equipment Company Ltd.
Conway, A. C., Department of Industry
Cooke, M. A., CAP Ltd.
Cooper, N. H. R., University of Sussex
Cowling, V., International Computers Ltd.
Crapnell, L. A., Ferranti Ltd.
Cutts, D. L., Imperial Group Ltd.
Davies, B. S., Bank of England
Duhig, A. J., John Hoskyns & Company Ltd.
Dumayne, J., The Peninsular & Oriental Steam Navigation Company
Dunnet, J. F., American Express IBC
El-Mosawi, A., Logica Ltd.
Evans, B. G., British Gas

Evans, D., Control Data Ltd.
Fasey, M. D. P., Admiralty Research Laboratory
Fedden, D. C., ICI Ltd.
Flinders, M. D., Philips Industries CISA
Fordred, B. J., ICL Dataskil
Forster, D. J., Shell International Petrolium Co. Ltd.
Fox, J., F International
Foxley, E., University of Nottingham
Frewin, J., National Development Programme for Computer-Assisted
     Learning
Gellatly, J. P., Peat Marwick Mitchell & Co.
Gibby, D. R., SHAPE Technical Centre
Gilchrist, H., Civil Service Department
Glancy, H., Civil Service Department
Greggains, D. J. K., Unilever Ltd.
Grosswell, L. O., Arvld Nilsson AS
Hare, K. J., Post Office Data Processing Service
Harris, M., J Sainsbury
Hart, C. J., ICL
Hayes, A. F., British Steel Corporation
Hayward, M. L., Hawker Siddley Aviation Ltd.
Haywood, C. B., Burroughs Machines Ltd.
Heath, R., Dataweek
Helks, J. R., Computer Power
Hernstrom, L. G., Mjolkcentralen
Hockley, L. C., Burroughs Machines Ltd.
Huckle, Dr. P. R., IBM (UK) Ltd.
Jackson, K., Peat Marwick Mitchell & Co.
Jeffereys, R., Burroughs Machines Ltd.
Jeffery, N. A. H., ICL
Jones, C., Transcripta Books
Jones, T. T., IBM (UK) Ltd.
Kanauros, E., Dickenson Robinson Group
Kenny, P., SPL International
Kingscott, T. F., IMI Ltd.
Kirkham, J. W., North Thames Gas
Knowles, R. D. F., TSB Computer Group
Knowles, T., GEC Computers Ltd.
Lavington, Dr. S. H., The University, Manchester
Lever, J., Hatfield Polytechnic
Linter, D. E., Ministry of Defence
Lewin, E., International Computers Ltd.
Mathews, F. D., Legal & General Assurance Scty. Ltd.

Miles, C. H., International Computers Nederland BV
Miners, J. S., Massey Ferguson Manfg. Co.
Moore, D. I., Massey Ferguson Manfg. Co.
Neve, N. J. F., Royal Radar Establishment
Nicholls, B. A., International Computers Ltd.
O'Connell, G. T., Bis-Brandon Applied Systems
O'Shea, M., Imperial College
Pavelin, Dr. C. J., Atlas Computer Laboratory
Peach, D. E., AUWE
Pollam, G., J Sainsbury
Pyne, R., Computing
Rachlin, A. H., Software Sciences
Rappaport, P. J., ICL
Ratcliffe, W. C., Westinghouse Brake & Signal Co. Ltd.
Reagan, R., ICI Ltd.
Reed, W., Ministry of Defence (Navy)
Richings, G. W., Bis-Brandon
Roberts, M. G., British Gas Corporation
Roberts, P. D., University of York
Roberts-Jones, J. M., Liverpool City Council
Shaida, H., Plessey Co. Ltd.
Sharp, J., British Gas Corporation
Sime, Dr. J. G., University of Glasgow
Sinclair, D., Department of the Environment
Smallbone, J. D., Institute of Oceanographic Sciences
Smith, B. L., British Gas Corporation
Smith, J. P., The Peninsular & Oriental Steam Navigation Company
Smith, W., British Steel Corporation
Smyth, P. J. A., Pirelli SPA
Southgate, A., British Gas Corporation
Spriggs, J., Post Office Processing Service
Stade, W. H., Siemens AG
Stevenson, M. G., National Cash Register Company Ltd.
Stross, C. O. M., Hawker Siddley Aviation Ltd.
Tanqueray, D., Control Data Ltd.
Thomas, D. E., Ministry of Defence
Thrussell, C., J Sainsbury
Tindall, D., East Midlands Electricity Board
Trout, R. G., Atkins Computing Services Ltd.
Tupman, A. G., GEC Computers Ltd.
Van Tue, M. T., Institut National Astronomie, Centre de Calcul
    Geophysique
Verbist, G. L. G., IBM Belgium

Vinyard, V. C., Fisons Limited
Walker, F., Annan Impey Morrish
Walker, W. A., Ministry of Defence (Navy)
Ward, J. T., The Prudential Assurance Company Ltd.
Wates, M. P., PA Management Consultants
Webb, N. H. J., Solicitor's Law
Weiis, E. M. B., International Computers Nederland BV
Widger, G. F. T., Deloitte Robson Morrow & Co.
Wilks, G., Department of the Environment
Willars, H. E., Bohlin & Stromberg AB
Wilsdon, A. I., Plessey Radar Limited
Wilson, A. R., Massey Ferguson Manfg. Co.
Wood, W. F., International Computers Limited
Wright, B. W., Burmah-Castrol
Wright, J. O., Prudential Assurance Company Ltd.

Appendix B: Corporations, Organizations, and Manufacturers Named in This Book

UNITED KINGDOM-BASED ORGANIZATIONS

Admiralty Research Laboratory, Teddington, Middlesex
Annan Impey & Morrish, London
Arthur Andersen & Company, London
Atlas Laboratory, Chilton, Berkshire
The Atomic Energy Research Establishment, Harwell, Berkshire
British Computer Society (BCS), London
British Gas, London
Central Computer Agency (CCA), London
GEC Computers Ltd., London
ICL Systems, Reading, Berkshire
Institute of Oceanographic Sciences (IOS), Godalming, Surrey
Mitre Corporation
National Physical Laboratory (NPL), Teddington, Middlesex
Peat Marwick & Mitchell, London
Post Office Telecommunications, London
Software Sciences Limited, Farnborough, Hampshire

MULTINATIONAL COMPANIES

American Express International Banking Corporation
Burroughs Machines, Ltd.

Control Data Corporation (CDC)
Honeywell
International Business Machines (IBM)
The Rand Corporation
Rank Xerox
Unilever
Univac

Appendix C: A Benchmark Program

```
begin
        real    x1, x2, x3, x4, x, y, z, t, t1, t2;
        array   e1[1:4];
        integer  i, j, k, l, n1, n2, n3, n4, n5, n6, n7, n8, n9, n10, n11,
                n12;

        procedure   pa (e);
        array   e;
        begin integer   j;
                j:=0;
           lab: e[1]:=(e[1]+e[2]+e[3]-e[4])*t;
                e[2]:=(e[1]+e[2]-e[3]+e[4])*t;
                e[3]:=(e[1]-e[2]+e[3]+e[4])*t;
                e[4]:=(-e[1]+e[2]+e[3]+e[4])/t2;
                j:=j+1;
                if j<6 then go to lab;
        end    procedure pa;

        procedure   p0;
        begin   e1[j]:=e1[k];
                e1[k]:=e1[1];
                e1[1]:=e1[j];
        end    procedure p0;

        procedure p3(x,y,z);
        value   x,y;        real x,y,z;
        begin   x:=t*(x+y);
                y:=t*(x+y);
```

169

```
        z:=(x+y)/2;
end    procedure p3;

procedure   pout (n, j, k, x1, x2, x3, x4);
value   n, j, k, x1, x2, x3, x4;
integer   n, j, k;      real x1, x2, x3, x4;
begin
```

comment   this procedure prints out the values of n, j, k, x1, x2, x3
          and x4: format and medium are unimportant;

```
          outinteger (1, n);    outinteger (1, j);    outinteger (1, k);
              outreal (1, x1);      outreal (1, x2);
              outreal (1, x3);      outreal (1, x4),
end    procedure pout;
```

comment   initialize constants:
```
          t:=0.499975;    t1:=0.50025;    t2:=2.0;
```

comment   read value of i, controlling total weight;
          if i=10 the total weight is one million Whetstone instructions;
```
          ininteger (0, i);
```

comment   set values of module weights;
```
          n1:=       0;        n7:=  32*i;
          n2:= 12* i;          n8:=899*i;
          n3:= 14* i;          n9:=616*i;
          n4:=345* i;          n10:=    0;
          n5:=       0;        n11:=  93*i;
          n6:=210* i;          n12:=    0;
```

comment   module 1: simple identifiers;
```
          x1:=1.0;      x2:=x3:=x4:=-1.0;
          for   i:=1    step 1 until n1 do
          begin   x1:=(x1+x2+x3-x4)*t;
                  x2:=(x1+x2-x3+x4)*t;
                  x3:=(x1-x2+x3+x4)*t;
                  x4:=(-x1+x2+x3+x4)*t;
          end    module 1;
          pout (n1, n1, n1, x1, x2, x3, x4);
```

comment   module 2: array elements;
```
          e1[1]:=1.0;      e1[2]:=e1[3]:=e1[4]:=- 1.0;
          for   i:=1    step 1 until n2 do
          begin   e1[1]:=(e1[1]+e1[2]+e1[3]-e1[4])*t;
                  e1[2]:=(e1[1]+e1[2]-e1[3]+e1[4])*t;
                  e1[3]:=(e1[1]-e1[2]+e1[3]+e1[4])*t;
                  e1[4]:=(-e1[1]+e1[2]+e1[3]+e1[4])*t;
```

end   module 2;
pout (n2, n3, n2, e1[1], e1[2], e1[3], e1[4]);

comment   module 3: array as parameter;
    for   i:=1   *step* 1 *until* n3 *do*
    pa (e1);
    pout (n3, n2, n2, e1[1], e1[2], e1[3], e1[4]);

comment   module 4: conditional jumps;
    j:=1;
    for   i:=1   *step* 1 *until* n4 *do*
    begin   *if* j=1 *then* j:=2 *else* j:=3;
            if j>2 *then* j:=0 *else* j:=1;
            if j<1 *then* j:=1 *else* j:=0;
    end   module 4;
    pout (n4, j, j, x1, x2, x3, x4);

comment   module 5: omitted;

comment   module 6: integer arithmetic;
    j:=1;   k:=2;   l:=3;
    for   i:=1   *step* 1 *until* n6 *do*
    begin   j:=j*(k−j)*(l−k);
           k:=l*k−(l−j)*k;
           l:=(l−k)*(k+j);
           e1[l−1]:=j+k+l;
           e1[k−1]:=j*k*l;
    end   module 6;
    pout (n6, j, k, e1[1], e1[2], e1[3], e1[4]);

comment   module 7: trig. functions;
    x:=y:=0.5;
    for   i:=1   *step* 1 *until* n7 *do*
    begin
    x:=t*arctan(t2*sin(x)*cos(x)/(cos(x+y)+cos(x−y)−1.0));
    y:=t*arctan(t2*sin(y)*cos(y)/(cos(x+y)+cos(x−y)−1.0));
    end   module 7;
    pout (n7, j, k, x, x, y, y);

comment   module 8: procedure calls;
    x:=y:=z:=1.0;
    for   i:=1   *step* 1 *until* n8 *do*
    p3 (x, y, z);
    pout (n8, j, k, x, y, z, z);

comment   module 9: array references;
    j:=1;   k:=2;   l:=3;

```
        e1[1]:=1.0;        e1[2]:=2.0;        e1[3]:=3.0;
        for   i:=1    step 1 until n9 do
        p0;
        pout (n9, j, k, e1[1], e1[2], e1[3], e1[4];
```

comment   module 10: integer arithmetic;
```
        j:=2;        k:=3;
        for   i:=1    step 1 until n10 do
        begin   j:=j+k;
                k:=j+k;
                j:=k−j;
                k:=k−j−j;
        end   module 10;
        pout (n10, j, k, x1, x2, x3, x4);
```

comment   module 11: standard functions;
```
        x:=0.75;
        for   i:=1    step 1 until n11 do
        x:=sqrt(exp(ln(x)/t1));
        pout (n11, j, k, x, x, x, x);
```
end

Appendix D: C. M. Berners-Lee's Later Work

Since the talk was given, considerable further progress has been made, and what follows is taken from more recent use of the techniques described in my Benchmarking '74 paper. They include a more comprehensive statistical analysis of the accuracy of model predictions than was available at the time of the original paper and better methods for setting up the model.

Figure 1 shows the output of the system measurement and modeling utility used for this purpose. The measurements taken from the system monitoring file are displayed averaged over a fixed period corresponding to one horizontal space on the printout. At the top of the figure the CPU utilization is shown (dots), with the object program (stars) underneath. Next comes operating system activity measured in chapter changes per unit time scaled for the power of the processor. This is followed by total file store transfers, further broken down by spindles ("Unit Number Transfers"). At the bottom is the number of background jobs and MOP jobs. A proportion of these have core images. A smaller proportion (about half) have a slot in the CPU schedule.

The model assumes that the level of multi-processing is proportional to the number of core images. In this case, the constant of proportionality has been taken as 0.5. For each time period, the model's estimate of the time to process the system traffic (for the CPU and devices) is compared with the length of the period. This ratio is known as the time ratio, and ten times its value is displayed as a character, "A" thus corresponding to a value of the time ratio between 0.95 and 1.05. It will be seen that in this case an accuracy

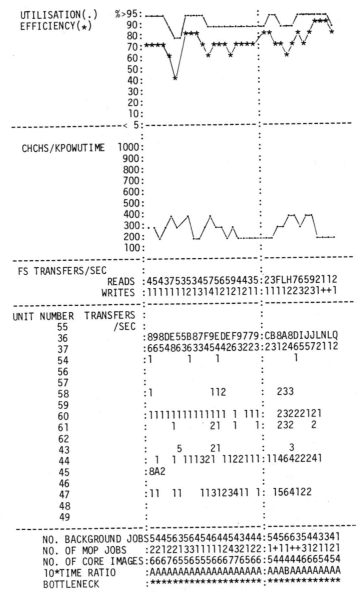

FIG. 1   Validation of model results.

of better than five percent is attained almost throughout. It is, of course, easy to model the throughput accurately when the CPU utilization is very high, as it is throughout most of the period shown. The really encouraging part of this printout is the high accuracy maintained through the periods when the CPU utilization is relatively low, because this shows that the model is accurately reflecting the effect of the CPU being kept waiting by peripheral queuing. These recent results are much better than those reported in the original talk, where only about half the time ratios were in the "A" category.

Appendix E: A Challenge to Benchmarking

P. J. Kiviat

*Federal Computer Performance Evaluation
and Simulation Center (FEDSIM)*

During the last eight years my career has changed direction in many ways: I am no longer a researcher; I now have a responsibility for producing results, rather than talking about how results might be produced more efficiently; my focus has narrowed from a concern with models of all varieties of systems to models of only computer systems; and my focus has widened to include techniques other than simulation. Officially, I am the technical director of an organization that is an internal supplier of computer performance evaluation and computer system simulation services to agencies of the U.S. government. To place this in some perspective, at the close of our 1973 fiscal year, the general management category of computers numbered 7,149.

Since benchmarking in its various forms is a computer performance evaluation (CPE) technique combining aspects of both measurement and prediction, my organization is presently very much involved with it and its many problems. Simply put, a benchmark is a system "stimulator" that is intended to cause a predetermined load on one or more components of a system for the purposes of:

1. Functional demonstration
2. analytical study (measurement)
3. performance demonstration (prediction)

Benchmarks serve definite, specific and different purposes.

Let me illustrate some of our present difficulties with a few examples:

How do you describe a workload?

- How do you summarize capacity usage?
- How do you compare two workloads?

At Benchmarking '74 we were told that there are only eight or nine possible programs or workloads. Let's assume that's true. What scale have we to enable us to tell which workload category we have? We haven't one.

How do you select "representative" benchmark programs?

- How do you isolate significant programs?
- How do you accommodate variability?
- What are measures of significance?

How do you represent workloads?

- Do you use real programs?
- Do you use standard benchmarks?
- Do you use synthetic programs?

How do you deal with "impossible" situations?

- We cannot configure and test large numbers of interactive terminals
- We cannot test nonexistent software (DMS)
- We cannot prevent manufacturer's tuning of benchmark programs

How do you deal with the natural tension that exists between a manufacturer who wants to optimize his benchmark and the user who wants him to run it the way a "normal" programmer would?

Some of these problems are more important than others in some benchmarking contexts. For example, the use of benchmarking for computer system selection poses more severe problems than the use of benchmarking for analytical system studies. Particular problems are:

The cost to vendors and users

The use of artificial stimulators (emulators) for terminals has implications for vendor protests

To address these and other important issues in the United States we've established several committees and groups, some of them ad hoc in nature and some of them officially formed organizations. The National Bureau of Standards has a task group on workload definition and benchmarking that is addressing the subjects of defining workloads and benchmarking practices. Are there any possible standards? They're in the process of issuing guidelines, not standards, because they feel that it's presumptuous to think we have standards for running benchmarks today. Guidelines that are management oriented and that will help people conduct better benchmarks should make our manufacturer friends happy because they say some very simple things that are too often ignored. For example: "Test the benchmark before you give it to the manufacturer." "Read the tape before you send it so you know there's something on it." We hope to reduce the cost of benchmarking by the distribution of rather practical and pragmatic guidelines!

The United States Air Force and the Mitre Corporation are working on the development of a remote terminal emulator, a minicomputer-driven device that can simulate, or emulate, depending upon which term you like, hundreds of computer terminals connected to some host computer. It may make possible the stimulation of a computer by hundreds of devices and not just the few that are used today.

The U.S. Army has a group working on standard benchmarks. In the belief that, just as there may be only eight or nine different situations that computers find themselves involved with, there is some limited number of program modules that is the basis of all programming, a group was formed to discover them and write standard programs that you could put together (having had them pretested) and come up with a flexible and inexpensive benchmark. This group is now looking for these modules.

The General Services Administration is sponsoring new ideas in the procurement process. They realize that the ultimate procurement technique will not be a purely technical one, in all likelihood, as we're not going to come up with the perfect technical device to do benchmarking, whether it's hardware or software. They recently issued a request for proposal for a large multi-access system that said in essence to the vendors: "Run the benchmark this way: Configure three terminals. We will give you a magnetic tape containing the workload of some larger number of terminals. You can use any device you wish to read this tape and deliver the workload to the CPU through a front-end processor. That's the way you have to show the system works during the benchmark demonstration." They also had to run this simulated workload in a specified amount of time. The "kicker" was that when the system was actually delivered, and before it was accepted, the vendor had to install all the terminals and reproduce the benchmark workload within 10 percent of the benchmarking time. If they couldn't do this, the system was not accepted.

I'm one of the school who believes that some combination of benchmarking and contractual obligation making a manufacturer liable for meeting the performance that he claims he can meet is the best practical procurement practice. You need the benchmark to establish credibility and to select those manufacturers that have a reasonable chance of performing from those who are trying to buy their way in. But, given that screening device, let the manufacturer decide how much risk he wants to absorb. If he wants to install a system that won't work, that's his problem, as long as he has to deliver enough equipment contractually to make it work.

We at FEDSIM employ a variety of "tools" in our benchmark-oriented activities. We use measurement—both hardware and software measurement—extensively to classify programs and select programs. We also use accounting data extensively. Our staff is currently working on something that they call a *Resource Consumption Index*, which uses measurement data to classify and select important programs from workloads and thereby form benchmarks. As we are interested in consolidating computer systems, there's always the question of comparing the workloads of systems from different manufacturers in different environments. We're trying to use measurement data with an algorithmic approach to combining different measurements, using weighting factors such as instruction counts and price of components to come up with a machine-independent and site-independent measure of workload. Whether it will succeed I don't know, but I have hopes for it.

We use simulation a great deal for testing the representativeness of benchmarks. We may simulate an entire workload, then simulate a selected benchmark set to see whether or not the resource consumption of the benchmark set is the same as the resource consumption of the workload. In this way, we get a better feeling for just how representative these workloads are that we give to manufacturers. We also use simulation to set performance criteria for requests for proposals. If a manufacturer is asked to run a certain workload within 50 minutes, we'd like to know that it really doesn't take two hours. That has happened. Realism is important, and we use simulation to try and set realistic performance goals. We also use simulation to extend benchmarks to those areas that cannot be tested, such as large multi-access systems. There is a U.S. government procurement regulation that says that simulation cannot be used as a sole selection criterion. Simulation can only be used in conjunction with other methods, which is how we use it. I don't believe that any simulator is accurate enough to make what is a very important binding determination as to whose computer performs the best.

This is what we're doing at FEDSIM today, plus a small amount of research to try and solve the problems of tomorrow, some of which I'll list now; the kinds of things we have in our future that will make our lives even more difficult than they are at present, if you can imagine that.

How do we handle distributed systems? Highly modularized and self-organizing systems? How do we measure systems whereby the whole CPU is on one chip that we can't even see, much less attach a hardware monitor probe to? What do we do when the dynamics of innovation is faster than the policies we can implement to react to those innovations? How do we deal with systems that have human interference in the form of real-time interaction? In the old days you could model a standard batch system very easily. I can't conceive of modeling, whether through a benchmark or a simulator, some of the systems that will be coming up in the next five or ten years. So the problems we're talking about today are really simple problems. We just don't realize how simple they are.

We have a challenge before us: To produce techniques and procedures for developing an understanding of and predicting the performance of computer systems. It's my challenge, because of the organization I'm with, and I think it's your challenge too.

Bibliography

Adiri, I. 1969. A time-sharing queue with a finite number of customers. *Journal of the Association for Computing Machinery* 16:315.

Bell, T. 1974. SHARE—computer measurement and evaluation proceedings. Vol. 2. New York: SHARE Inc.

Berners-Lee, C. M. 1973. A paper on computer performance. Paper read at an On-line Conference, Brunel University, U.K.

Blatny, J., Clark, S. R., and Rourke, T. A. 1972. On the optimization of performance of time sharing systems by simulation. *Communications of the Association for Computing Machinery* 15:411.

Buchholz, W. 1969. A synthetic job for measuring system performance. *IBM System Journal* 8(4):309–318.

Clark, R. J., and Wisniewska, A. S. 1971. The ICL Real Time Model. Paper read at NATO-APOR Conference.

Cussons, C. J., and Broadribb, J. P. 1973. A configuration modelling system. Paper read at an On-line conference, 17–19 September 1973, at Brunel University, U.K.

Emery, G. 1968. *Electronic data processing.* London: Pitman.

Fine, G. H., and McIsaac, P. V. 1965. Simulation of a time-sharing system. *Management Science* 12:B180.

Freiberger, W. 1972. *Statistical computer performance evaluation.* New York: Academic Press.

Goff, N. S. 1973. The case for benchmarking. *Computers and Automation* 22(5):23–25.

Greenberger, M. 1971. Performance Evaluation and Monitoring. *Computer Surveys* 3:79.

Houldsworth, D., Robinson, G. W., and Wells, M. 1973. A multi-terminal benchmark. *Software—Practice and Experience* 3:43.

Hughes, P. H. 1974. *Infotech—State of the art, report 18.* Maidenhead, Berkshire: Infotech Information Ltd.

Ihrer, F. C. 1972. Benchmarking vs. simulation. *Computers and Automation* 21(11):8–10.

Kilgannon, P. 1972. *The student's systems analysis.* London: Edward Arnold.

Knuth, D. E. 1971. An empirical study of Fortran programs. *Software—Practice and Experience* 1(2):105–133.

Krishnamoorthi, B., and Wood, R. C. 1966. Time-shared computer operations with both inter arrival and service times exponential. *Journal of the Association for Computing Machinery* 13:317.

Lucas, H. C. 1971. Performance evaluation and monitoring. *Computing Surveys* 3:79.

Nielson, N. R. 1967. The simulation of time-sharing systems. *Communications of the Association for Computing Machinery* 10:397.

Randell, B., and Russell, L. J. 1964. *Algol 60 Implementation.* Automatic Programming Information Centre Studies in Data Processing, No. 5. New York: Academic Press.

Scherr, A. L. 1965. "An analysis of time-shared computer systems." Ph.D. dissertation MACTR18, Massachusetts Institute of Technology, Cambridge, Massachusetts.

Sutcliffe, S. E. 1972. "On the design of multi-purpose systems." Ph.D. thesis, University of Manchester Institute of Science and Technology, U.K.

————— 1973. Selecting the components of multi-purpose computer systems. In *Proceedings of the International Computing Symposium*, ed. A. Gunther et al., pp. 187–193. Davos, Switzerland: North Holland Publications Company.

Thomas, R. E., and Kent, P. 1972. Control of queues in a permissive society. *Software— Practice and Experience* 2:79.

Webb, M. H. J. 1972. Computer procurement policies for universities and similar users. *Computer Journal* 15(2):170–175.

Wichmann, B. A. 1973. *Algol 60 compilation and assessment*. New York: Academic Press.

Wickens, R. F. 1968. A brief review of computer assessment methods. *Radio Electronic Engineering (GB)* 36(5):285–87.

Index